Contents

KV-192-385

Word-List

apartheid:
a system of government used in South Africa where white and black peoples are to have separate development

austerity:
a period of severe hardship in Britain after the Second World War

autonomy:
the right of self-government or personal freedom

capitalism:
an economic system where the means of production (industry, power etc) are owned by one class, the capitalists, for their own profit

civil rights:
the right of people to vote, to be elected into office and to be free to move, speak and worship

Cold War:
the rivalry after 1945 between the USSR and communist states, and the USA and countries of western Europe

communism:
either (1) a state or government where property is owned by the people as a whole, or (2) a revolutionary movement which seeks to overthrow the capitalist or other system of government

Commonwealth:
the organisation composed of Britain and the former dominions and colonies

commune:
a system of land ownership practised in China where the land, equipment and all produce are shared in common by a group of workers

counter-revolution:
where a group or political party seeks to overthrow the government set up as the result of a revolution

democracy:
a system of government where people, by voting in elections, have control over the government

deflation:
where the spending power of people is reduced by means of heavy taxation

détente:
the ending of a period of hostile feelings between two or more states

devaluation:
to reduce the value of one currency (the pound) against another (the dollar)

free trade:
where there are no or very few controls over trade

immigration:
people entering one country from another, and intending to settle there

imperialism:
a system of empire, where one country rules over others

inflation:
where prices (and sometimes wages) are rising rapidly

Iron Curtain:
the frontier or dividing line between communist states of eastern Europe and the western nations, after 1945

mandates:
where a country (the mandate) is ruled over by another until it has been prepared for independence

marxism:
the political ideas and system of government designed by Karl Marx

nationalization:
where the state takes control (as in the coal industry, Britain, 1947)

nationalism:
where one country's aims are to be strong and independent of other nations

referendum:
a vote taken in a country where a single question is asked, and the answer is usually 'yes' or 'no'

socialism:
a system where the economic power of a country is planned by the state and where the main aim is the general welfare of all the people

'stop-go':
where the economy of a country (i.e. Britain) is inflation followed by deflation

sterling crisis:
where British pounds are sold in foreign exchange markets to buy other currencies, so causing a fall in the value of the pound

tariffs:
customs duties paid on imports or exports

Warsaw Pact:
the defence system set up in 1955 between the USSR and eastern European states

Zionism:
the movement to establish a Jewish homeland

Introduction

For the Pupils—How to Use this Book

20th Century World History is made up of two books. One book is about the period of history from 1900 to 1945 and includes accounts of the First and Second World Wars. The second book deals with events throughout the world since 1945. Most of the important political events of these years are described in the books. They are about the world leaders who deeply influenced what happened—Mao Tse-tung, Stalin and Khrushchev, Truman and Kennedy, de Gaulle, Gandhi and many others. The books are also about wars, peace treaties, the United Nations and its work, the main social changes in these years, and the economic changes that have brought prosperity to some and poverty to others.

The books have been designed to help you with your studies and examinations. There is information about the main events, and there are also maps, drawings, diagrams and pictures to help to explain what happened. Lastly, there are questions for you to answer. The information that you need to answer these questions is mainly provided in the text, or in maps and pictures. Sometimes you will have to read more about the topic in another book. The questions that you have to answer are based on questions set by Examination Boards such as those which set CSE examinations. You should have a looseleaf file or a notebook in which to write your answers, and to draw the maps and diagrams. All the questions which you have to answer appear in boxes and are printed in smaller type like this:

> Draw a map to show the advance of the communist forces in Korea.

Words used in the book
Some words used in the book, such as 'communism', 'inflation' and 'austerity' are sometimes difficult to understand. On the opposite page there is a *word-list* which gives these words with an explanation of their meaning.

The Hungarian Revolution, 1956. When the Russians abandoned their tanks in the streets of Budapest, revolutionaries wrote the sign of free Hungary on the tanks

1 The End of the War

In May 1945 the Second World War came to
an end in Europe. At last, Germany had been
defeated but at a terrible cost. Over 30 million
people had died; cities lay in ruins; complete
industrial regions had been destroyed; farms
and fields were deserted. In Germany, the
Allied soldiers put down their rifles in order to
carry food to the starving people. In Russia, 25
million were homeless, and the Soviet leaders,
like other Governments, faced the enormous
task of recovery.

In August 1945, after American planes
dropped atom bombs on Hiroshima and
Nagasaki, Japan surrendered. As in Europe,
American troops occupied the lands of a defeated enemy, and straightaway had to deal
with many problems.

The Peace Conferences

At the Yalta Conference in February 1945, the
Allied leaders met to decide what should happen to the territories seized by Germany during
the war. The Russian leader, Stalin, wanted to
protect the USSR from any further attack by
forming a 'buffer' zone in eastern Europe. He
also wanted to punish and cripple Germany.
President Roosevelt hoped the USA would
take a lead in keeping peace throughout the
world. He also wanted other nations to adopt a
policy of 'free trade' so that American goods
could be exported. Winston Churchill, the
British Prime Minister, hoped to check the
power of the USSR by continuing the wartime
alliance. But President Roosevelt died in April
1945 and when the 'Big Three' met in July,
Harry Truman was President. In addition,
Clement Attlee, the Labour leader, had become Prime Minister of Britain. At this conference, held at Potsdam in Germany, the
USSR's 1939 frontier (including former Polish
lands) was agreed on.

The city of Dresden (now in East Germany) in 1945,
almost completely destroyed by Allied bombers

The Allied leaders at Potsdam: Attlee, Truman and
Stalin (seated, left to right)

The Fate of Germany

At Potsdam, it was decided that Germany should be divided into four zones, French, British, American and Russian. The capital city, Berlin, was also divided into four parts. The western Allies hoped to keep Germany divided for only a short time. They planned a 'safe' Germany without any army and with a democratic form of government. Stalin, however, had other ideas. He wanted reparations from Germany, payment in goods for the damage caused by the war. He also intended to keep Germany weak, to ensure that there would be no further danger to the USSR.

The Nazi leaders who had survived the war were brought to trial at Nuremberg, accused of many crimes. Goering committed suicide, some were hanged and others were given long terms of imprisonment. The German people, crushed by war and horrified by news of what had happened in concentration camps, turned to their new democratic leaders.

Poland

The borders of Poland caused one of the first quarrels between the Allies. The Poles had been forced to give up lands in the east to the USSR. To compensate Poland, a large area of what had been German territory was added to the new Poland (*see the map*). The rivers Oder and Neisse now marked the border with Germany. Most of the nine million Germans who lived in this region fled or were deported as the Poles moved in. The USA and Britain could do nothing to stop this massive transfer of territory and people, and they had no choice but to agree.

Eastern Europe

The former allies of Nazi Germany were all dealt with in other peace treaties. In 1945, Austria was (like Germany) divided into four zones. In 1947, a series of peace treaties were signed with Rumania, Hungary and Bulgaria. The USSR was again the gainer. The Russians seized territory and industrial goods, and obtained the right to put troops in these countries.

German territory, 1939, transferred to Poland in 1945
German Democratic Republic [East Germany]
Federal German Republic [West Germany]

Germany and Poland in 1945

 'Germany will never again threaten her neighbours or the peace of the world'.
Potsdam Declaration, 1945

1 Draw or trace a map to show the new borders in 1945 of Germany and Poland. With different coloured pencils, shade in the four occupation zones in Germany and Austria.
2 In your notebook, write the heading 'The Peace Conferences'. Make a list of the major decisions taken by the Allied leaders at Yalta and Potsdam.
3 What did the Allied leaders do to ensure that Germany 'will never again threaten her neighbours'?

The United Nations

In 1945 the 'Big Three' who met at Yalta decided that there must be a new international organization. It should, they said, have real powers, unlike the League of Nations which had failed to prevent the Second World War. In June 1945, therefore, representatives of 50 nations met at San Francisco in the USA and set up the United Nations.

The main duty of the UN was to prevent war. If any dispute occurred between two or more states, the United Nations was to try to stop the fighting. If necessary, it was agreed that the UN could intervene to protect the victim of an attack. The leading statesmen of the world then signed the Charter of the UN and agreed that its main headquarters should be in New York.

The Far East

It had been decided in 1943 that the Japanese, when defeated, would lose all the territories that they had seized since 1894. Stalin also demanded 'special rights' in China, Mongolia and Manchuria. The Allied leaders gave in to Stalin who promised to bring the USSR into the war with Japan three months after the war with Germany had come to an end.

In 1945, American troops, commanded by General MacArthur, occupied Japan. The work of forming a new government was taken on by the Americans. Japan was therefore completely under American control. But in Mongolia a regime loyal to the USSR was very soon set up. In China itself, the forces of Chiang Kai-shek replaced the Japanese, but they soon came under pressure from the communists of Mao Tse-tung.

‘The purposes of the United Nations are to maintain international peace and security. . . .’
Charter of the United Nations, 1945

4 Write down three reasons to explain why world statesmen were so keen to set up the United Nations in 1945.

New York: the United Nations building stands, like a domino, in the left, foreground

The Communist Take-over in Eastern Europe

In 1945 the Russians took over the former independent countries of Estonia, Latvia and Lithuania which became parts of the USSR. Territory was also taken from Rumania (Bessarabia) and from Poland. A large part of eastern Poland, where millions of Russians and Ukrainians lived, was absorbed into the USSR.

As the Red Army marched across eastern Europe in 1945, the communists seized control. The leaders of the communist parties of Rumania, Bulgaria, Hungary and Czechoslovakia had been trained in Moscow. As soon as they returned to their own countries, protected by Russian troops, they began to move into positions of power within the governments. At Yalta and at Potsdam, Stalin had persuaded the Allied leaders to allow 'friendly' governments to be set up. Two of the first countries to become solidly communist were Yugoslavia and Albania. The leaders of the resistance movements in these countries (Marshal Tito and Enver Hoxha) took power when the Germans were driven out in 1944 and 1945. In Poland, Hungary, Bulgaria and Rumania, the communist take-over was a little slower but by 1948 the non-communist leaders had all fled or were in prison. Czechoslovakia was the last country to become communist-controlled, shortly after Jan Masaryk, the Foreign Minister, had been found dead in a courtyard. By March 1948, the whole of eastern Europe was firmly under Russian and communist control.

Russian territorial gains

1 Finland
2 Estonia
3 Latvia
4 Lithuania
5 East Prussia
6 Poland
7 Ruthenia
8 Bukovina
9 Bessarabia

Soviet gains

Soviet dominated

Other communist governments

5 Draw or trace the map of eastern Europe to show the territorial gains made by the USSR between 1938 and 1945. With different colours, shade in the countries of eastern Europe that had communist-controlled governments by 1948.

2 The Cold War, 1945–55

The Iron Curtain

On 6 March 1946, in a speech in the USA, Winston Churchill described the Russian take-over in eastern Europe.

> ‘ A shadow has fallen upon the scenes so lately lighted by an Allied victory. . . . From Stettin on the Baltic to Trieste on the Adriatic, an iron curtain has descended.’

The 'iron curtain' was the dividing line between the communist countries of the East, and the nations of western Europe and the USA. Eventually the curtain became a steel one when the Russians erected fences to mark the frontier. This stopped the flow of refugees who had been moving steadily from east to west.

The 'Cold War' was the rivalry after 1945 between the USA and its allies and the USSR and other communist countries. There was no war in the sense of armies fighting each other. But on several occasions the USSR and the USA came very near to a 'hot' war.

One of the main reasons for the Cold War was the economic power of the western countries. The USSR had suffered so severely in the Second World War that Stalin knew it would take years to reach American standards. He seemed to believe that the USA had ambitions in Europe. Russia, he thought, must be on guard, ready to fight to prevent American domination of Europe by military or economic means.

On the other hand, the USA was just as suspicious. The Americans watched helplessly as one eastern European country after another set up communist governments. Nor did Russian troops leave these countries. They stayed on to help the new communist rulers.

Another cause of suspicion was the position of Germany. Stalin had no intention of allowing Germany to be united and strong again. On

Refugees hurry to leave eastern Germany in 1946

the other hand, the USA seemed to be ready to help German recovery.

The answer to the question 'who caused the Cold War?' depends therefore on whether one was a Russian or an American, British or Polish. At the time, in 1946 and for some years afterwards, people on each side of the iron curtain *thought* that the USSR or the USA intended to overrun Europe, and that was enough to cause a lot of trouble.

This cartoon from a Russian magazine shows the western allies hatching a new Germany, a new Nazi Germany, to be let loose against communism.

10

Steps in the Cold War

This diagram shows the main steps that led eventually to the East and West alliances.

1945–7	USSR takes control in eastern Europe
1946	Churchill's 'iron curtain' speech
1947	the Truman Doctrine and the Marshall Plan
Oct. 1947	USSR sets up the Cominform
1948	the communists seize control of Czechoslovakia
1948	civil war in Greece
1948–9	the Berlin air lift
April 1949	NATO is set up

The Truman Doctrine

When the Germans were driven from Greece in 1944, the communists and the royalists began to fight each other in a civil war. In March 1947, President Truman announced that the USA would aid 'free peoples' to resist threats 'by armed minorities or by outside pressure'. The President suspected the USSR of helping the communists. 'Millions of dollars' worth of food, equipment and arms were sent to Greece (and also to Turkey) and the communists were beaten. In the next few years this 'Doctrine' was applied many times: the USA would give aid to any government that opposed communism. To the USSR this seemed an aggressive act by the USA.

The Marshall Plan

In 1947 General George Marshall was put in charge of a Plan by which America would bring aid to Europe. Over 15 000 million dollars was made available to help 16 'free world' nations. To starving, ruined western Europe, Marshall Aid was very welcome. A new organization, the Organization of European Economic Cooperation, was set up to administer the aid. An offer of help was made by the OEEC to the communist nations, but the USSR refused to allow them to take part. Thus the gulf widened between the poorer nations of the East and the western states, helped by American money and equipment.

The Cominform

Possibly as an answer to the Marshall Plan, the USSR set up the Cominform in October 1947. This was an organization of all communist parties, pledged to speed the spread of communism throughout the world. To the Americans, the Cominform seemed more proof of the USSR's aggressive intentions. To Stalin, it was a form of defence against the West.

Hero or tyrant? Stalin votes in an election

1 In your notebook, write the title 'The Cold War'. Write two sentences about each of these:
   a) the Iron Curtain
   b) the reasons for the Cold War
   c) the Truman Doctrine
   d) Marshall Aid
2 Copy the diagram of the steps in the Cold War into your notebook. Two steps have been missed out. Put them into the diagram in the correct places.
   a) Yugoslavia expelled from the Cominform by the USSR, June 1948
   b) USSR explodes atom bomb, August 1949

11

The Berlin Airlift

In 1945, Berlin was divided into four zones, administered by the four main allies. In elections to the City Assembly in the western sector, the communists were defeated. In February 1948 the Foreign Ministers met in London to discuss Germany's future. The USSR was not invited. In June, the western powers brought in a new German currency called the Deutschmark. The Russians could see that this would help Germany to become even more prosperous and successful. West Berlin, made up of the three allied zones was an irritating sore, deep in East Germany.

In June the roads and railways between Berlin and the west were all closed and the city was completely cut off.

General Clay, the American commander in-chief in Germany, ordered all his transport aircraft into action. The two million people in West Berlin had to rely on the planes to bring in all their food, coal, clothing and raw materials, and on the return flight to carry out the products of their industries. The USA provided about 70 per cent of the aircraft: the other allies gave the rest. By September a stream of planes flying from different parts of Germany (*see the map*) were landing in Berlin at intervals of three minutes, all through the day and night.

The Russians tried to win over the West Berliners by offering extra rations in East Berlin. Few people took up the offer. Therefore the city's gas and electricity supply from the eastern zone was cut off. The Berliners answered this by building their own power stations.

For two months the aeroplanes carried the precious cargoes. The Russian actions in 'blockading' Berlin brought the possibility of open war instead of a cold war a little nearer.

American planes line up on the run-way

In April 1949 the western nations formed a new alliance—NATO. Faced with the knowledge that the USA might be prepared to fight in Europe, the USSR agreed to re-open the road and rail links, and in May 1949 the airlift came to an end.

> 'When Berlin falls, Western Germany will be next. If we mean to hold Germany against communism, we must not budge.'
> General Lucius Clay, US Commander in Berlin, July 1948

> 'The currency reform . . . is designed to strengthen the position of the big German capitalists. . . who paved the way for and unleashed the Second World War, and who are now binding Germany to foreign capitalists.'
> Soviet Military Administration Order. No. 111, June 1948

Greece and Yugoslavia

Marshall Aid was given to both Greece and Turkey. The Greek army was re-equipped and industry was assisted. Roads and railways were built, and new farming methods (helped by thousands of American tractors) were introduced. The civil war dragged on for three years and Stalin seemed to tire of it for he gave little help to the Greek communists. By 1949 the war had ended in a victory for the royalists.

In Yugoslavia, Marshal Tito wanted to be free from both the USSR and the USA. During 1947 he resisted Soviet orders, and in June 1948 the Yugoslav Communist Party was expelled from the Cominform. Stalin was probably tempted to invade Yugoslavia, but may have thought the USA would use the atom bomb to defend Tito. The USA gave the Yugoslavs military and economic aid but Tito managed to keep as free from American influence as he did from the Russians.

The New Alliances

In December 1947, Britain, France, Belgium, the Netherlands and Luxemburg joined together to form a military organization called the Brussels Treaty powers. In April 1949, the USA suggested a bigger alliance, the North Atlantic Treaty Organization (NATO), made up of 10 western European nations, Canada and the USA. If one member was attacked, the others would come to its aid. Later on, Greece and Turkey joined (in 1952) and West Germany (in 1955). This strong alliance, backed by the military strength of the USA, probably saved Europe from a Soviet take-over in the 'colder' part of the Cold War. Even so,

"IF WE DON'T LET HIM WORK, WHO'S GOING TO KEEP HIM!"

A cartoon in a British newspaper shows that the Allies intended to release Germany from its bonds in order to take an equal place in Europe.

NATO was never an equal opponent of the USSR in terms of armies. In 1950, NATO had only 14 army divisions; the USSR and her allies had 173 divisions. But the USA had the atom bomb in reserve, although the USSR in the 1950s also developed nuclear weapons.

The Warsaw Pact

The Russian reply to NATO was a communist alliance which in 1955 became known as the Warsaw Pact. By it, the USSR was allowed to keep troops in the member states.

By 1950, therefore, the Cold War had entered a fresh stage. Both sides had powerful alliances and both had the atom bomb. There was always a danger that a spark might set off another world war.

The Alliances

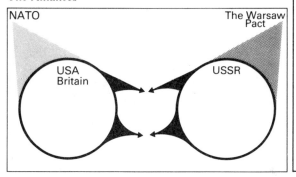

3 In your notebook, write out the reasons to explain why the Russians closed off communications by rail and road into West Berlin. Explain why they raised the blockade in May 1949.
4 Draw a map to show how the allies kept West Berlin supplied during the period of the blockade.
5 This diagram, showing the NATO and the Warsaw Pact powers, is unfinished. Copy the diagram into your notebook, and add the names of the missing countries. In NATO, 12 countries joined in 1949, and three others by 1955. In the Warsaw Pact were seven nations, excluding Albania which joined but left in 1961.

3 European Co-operation

Defence

At the end of the Second World War, people hoped that the nations would live peacefully together. However, as eastern Europe slipped into the hands of the communists, backed by a huge Russian army, the western powers grew anxious.

In March 1948, Britain, France, Holland, Belgium and Luxemburg signed the Treaty of Brussels. These nations agreed to combine together for their defence. At this time, these countries were very weak. If the Russians had attacked, they could have swept away the armies of the western nations.

As the 'iron curtain' came down over Europe, the Americans also became alarmed. When the road links with West Berlin were blocked in 1948, it looked as if the Russians were testing the determination of western Europe to stand up to communist pressure. At this point, the United States decided to join the western defence pact.

NATO

In April 1949, 12 nations signed a treaty that set up the North Atlantic Treaty Organization. Apart from the five Brussels Treaty countries, the USA, Canada, Iceland, Portugal, Norway, Denmark and Italy joined. Later on, Greece and Turkey joined, so making a ring of allies around the USSR. By the terms of the Treaty, the allies agreed to settle disputes by peaceful means, and to join together for their common defence.

Even so, in 1949, NATO was weak. The western powers had only 14 army divisions in Europe, compared with 200 Soviet divisions. On the other hand, the USA had the atomic bomb. But in 1950 Stalin gleefully said that the USSR also had the A-bomb.

In 1955 West Germany joined NATO and was allowed to have a separate army. The USSR (which had declared that NATO was 'a weapon of the capitalists') then formed the

Friends or enemies? General Montgomery, Commander-in-Chief at NATO, with Marshal Zhukov, Commander-in-Chief of the armies of the USSR

Warsaw Pact—a military alliance of eastern European countries under the Soviet umbrella.

> ' An armed attack against one or more of the nations in Europe or North America shall be considered as an attack against them all'.
> Section 5 of the North Atlantic Treaty, 1949

1 Draw or trace the map into your notebook to show the Warsaw Pact and NATO powers. Find out what happened at Cuba in 1962, and what the 'U2 incident' was in 1960. Explain how these events affected relations between the NATO powers and the USSR.

The military alliances of East and West, by 1962

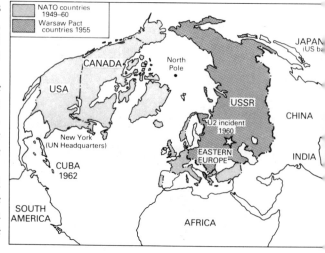

The 'New' Europe

'We must build a kind of United States of Europe'

Winston Churchill, 1946

In 1945 many people said that the nations of western Europe should continue to work together, as they had during the war. But at first it was all talk and no action. The most immediate and pressing job was the task of recovery—rebuilding shattered cities, roads, bridges, factories and so on.

The first kind of European co-operation came with Marshall Aid. The USA insisted that an organization should be set up to distribute the money and equipment to western Europe The *Organization for European Economic Co-operation* (OEEC) was set up in 1948 to get on with this job. The OEEC was the first real step in economic co-operation. The next stage came with NATO—a military alliance of the western powers—in 1949.

Some European leaders were not satisfied. One of them, a Frenchman called Jean Monnet, suggested the idea of a 'Community' of trading nations. In May 1950, the first step was taken by Robert Schuman, the Foreign Minister of France. He organized the formation in 1951 of the *European Coal and Steel Community* (ECSC). Six nations (France, West Germany, Italy, Belgium, Holland and Luxemburg) agreed to pool their efforts to produce and sell iron, steel and coal. During the next few years, the ECSC went from strength to strength. In 1955 the Foreign Ministers of these six nations met to explore other ways of co-operating. The British sent observers, who later withdrew from the discussions. A team of officials set to work to draft a new treaty to set up a 'Community' of trading nations.

The Common Market

In 1957 the 'Six' nations of the ECSC signed the Treaty of Rome. This set up the *European Economic Community* (EEC) which is often called 'The Common Market'. Britain refused to join. At the same time, an organization called *Euratom* (which had been set up to pool ideas and research into the peaceful uses of atomic energy) was brought under the control of the EEC.

The aims of the EEC partners, contained in the Treaty of Rome
- to abolish all tariffs and restrictions on trade
- to allow the free movement of goods, money and people
- a common trade policy towards other countries
- a common policy for farming and transport
- fair and free competition within the Community

The Community Building, the headquarters of the EEC, in Brussels

Britain—In or Out?

The Common Market was an instant success. From the moment it came into operation (1 January 1958) the trade of the six nations both with each other and with other nations increased.

Britain had decided not to join, largely because of trading agreements with the Commonwealth and the USA. Fearing to be left out in the cold, Britain in 1959 formed the *European Free Trade Association* (EFTA), made up of seven nations (Britain, Norway, Denmark, Austria, Sweden, Portugal and Switzerland). The aims of EFTA were less than those for EEC. EFTA agreed to reduce tariffs between the trading partners and to build up trade in various ways.

From the start, EEC was much more successful than EFTA. In 1963, the British, now realizing that they had slipped up in not joining, applied to become a member of the EEC. After long talks, President de Gaulle voted against Britain's entry. In 1967, Britain tried again, and was turned down for the second time. A third chance came when President de Gaulle retired, and in 1973, Britain (along with Ireland and Denmark) applied for membership and were admitted to the Common Market, and so the 'Six' became the 'Nine'. Even then, the British Labour Party still had doubts, and in 1975 a referendum, or national vote, was taken to see what people thought: the vote was strongly in favour of membership. EFTA was damaged by Britain's withdrawal, and after 1973 it had little influence.

Edward Heath, the British Prime Minister, speaks before signing the treaty for Britain's entry to the Common Market

	The original 'Six' nations of the European Economic Community, 1957
	The 'Six' become the 'Nine', 1973
	The Council of Mutual Economic Assistance in Eastern Europe (Comecon) 1949
	The European Free Trade Association, 1959–1973

2 In your notebook, write out the full titles of these organizations. Write lists of the member countries of each group. Explain what the aims were for each organisation.
   a) OEEC   b) ECSC
   c) EEC   d) EFTA

3 Draw a map in your notebook to show how the 'Six' became the 'Nine'. With a different colour, show the nations of Comecon, the communist trading organization.

The Work of the Community

The Parliaments and the Governments of the nine countries of EEC decide on the main lines of policy. The *Council of Ministers* (one Minister from each member country) take major decisions on, say, agricultural policies, or finance, or shipping. The *Commission* does the day-to-day running of the Community from the headquarters in Brussels. Over 8000 civil servants work for the Commission. They work under the Council of Ministers and see that their decisions are put into effect.

Another important section of the EEC is the *European Parliament*. Before 1979 the members of this Parliament were appointed by the Governments of the member states. However, since 1979 the members of the European Parliament are elected direct by voters in the nine countries. The Parliament has the right to question the policy decisions made and put into effect by the Commission. Another part of the EEC is the *Court of Justice*. It can deal with disputes and arguments between the member states.

In the first 10 years of the Common Market, trade between the member states more than trebled. The main reason for this success was that people in the 'Six' worked hard and produced high quality goods which they sold throughout the world. But there have also been problems and difficulties. In order to help European farmers (particularly French farmers) food prices have been high in the Community. This did not suit Britain which had a policy of 'cheap food'. By 1979, European farmers were producing huge surpluses of some crops and there were 'butter mountains' and 'apple mountains' at a time when people were starving in other parts of the world. In addition, it proved difficult to reach agreement in the EEC on fishing rights, on oil and gas production and other policies. Despite these problems, the EEC appears to have benefited the member nations because of the cooperation between them, and the help they have been able to give to weaker countries.

A French view of Britain's wish to join the Common Market (*right*)

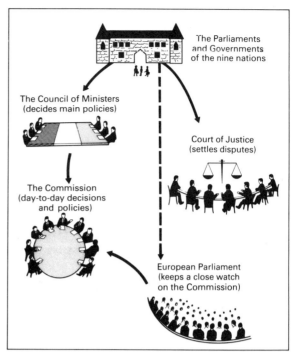

The Parliaments and Governments of the nine nations

The Council of Ministers (decides main policies)

Court of Justice (settles disputes)

The Commission (day-to-day decisions and policies)

European Parliament (keeps a close watch on the Commission)

The European Economic Community: how it works

4 Draw a diagram in your book to show how the different parts of the European Economic Community are linked together.
5 Write out the titles of these parts of the EEC and explain what each group does:
a) the Council of Ministers
b) the European Parliament
c) the Commission
d) the Court of Justice.
6 In your book, write out five advantages of belonging to the EEC. Then write down any disadvantages you can think of.

EUROPE DES 6

escaro.

17

4 France: de Gaulle and the 5th Republic

On 25 August 1944, General de Gaulle drove into Paris. Huge crowds lined the roads, cheering loudly and waving flags. De Gaulle had been in exile for four years, leading the Free French army and organizing the Resistance movement in the fight against Hitler's Germany. Outside the Ministry of War in Paris, his car stopped and he entered the office he had left in 1940. 'Not a piece of furniture, not a rug, not a curtain had been disturbed' he wrote later. 'I installed my staff at once and got down to work.'

But the war had not ended. On the night after de Gaulle's return, a German air attack on Paris killed over a thousand people. As the German army retreated, the fighting caused great damage to many French towns. The work of recovery began almost immediately. Industries, ruined by four years of war and occupation, had to be rebuilt. Coal, gas, electricity, transport and other industries were brought under government control. De Gaulle arranged elections to the first Assembly of the new 4th Republic. In the voting, the communists won 160 seats, making them the biggest of the political parties. Between them, de Gaulle's right-wing parties had only 66 seats. It was clear from the start the left-wing groups would make trouble for the General.

The 4th Republic

Quarrels broke out between de Gaulle and the politicians. In January 1946, he suddenly resigned, leaving Paris for his country home. For the next 12 years, the General lived in retirement, writing his memoirs.

In its early days the politicians of the 4th Republic faced many problems. Among them were:

- in Indo-China, fighting broke out between the communists, led by Ho Chi Minh, and the French army;
- in France, prices were high and food was scarce;
- French industry, damaged by the war, needed new equipment and money to invest;
- in politics, there were many different political parties which could not agree on a common policy.

In order to form a government, several of these parties formed a *coalition*, a government made up of several groups. If one party disagreed and left the coalition, the government usually collapsed. In ten years, there were twenty different governments in France. As a result, there was often great confusion in Paris, and this made recovery very difficult.

---

1 In your notebook, make a list of the difficulties faced by the 4th Republic from 1945 to 1958.

1945, the end of the road. French soldiers in the grounds of Hitler's house at Berchtesgaden in Bavaria

Roosevelt, de Gaulle and Churchill, the war leaders

Algeria

'There is a wind of change blowing through Africa.'
Harold Macmillan, British Prime Minister, 1960

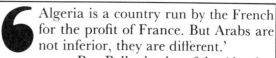
'Algeria is a country run by the French for the profit of France. But Arabs are not inferior, they are different.'
Ben Bella, leader of the Algerian National Liberation Front (FLN), 1958

Overseas, the French did not win any friends. In Indo-China, the war against the communists lasted for eight years and ended when the French army was defeated at Dien Bien Phu. The USA took over from the French in Vietnam, and the war went on.

In Morocco and Tunisia the French agreed to independence for these countries. But, in Algeria, there was to be no surrender.

France had ruled Algeria since 1830. The country was four times the size of France and had over a million French settlers. The Arabs had very little political power: they felt that their country was run entirely by and for Europeans. After 1948 the Arabs demanded independence and in 1954 Ben Bella formed the FLN to fight the French. But the French-Algerians, backed by the army and the Paris government, refused to give way. A civil war began, which lasted for seven years; it was marked by cruelties on both sides. The French accused other Arab states of helping the rebels and in 1956 French and British troops invaded the Suez Canal area in an attempt (which failed) to overthrow President Nasser of Egypt, who had been encouraging and helping the Algerian rebels.

In 1956 there was another complication. The French discovered large supplies of natural gas and oil in the Sahara, thus making Algeria more valuable. Over half a million French troops were sent to Algeria. The fighting became even more brutal, with both sides using murder and torture.

In 1957 it seemed as if the civil war in Algeria might spread to France. The army was determined to hang on to Algeria and for a time it looked as if the generals might seize power in Algiers or in Paris. In May 1958 mobs rioted in the streets of Algiers. The generals saw their chance and took over the government of Algeria. In Paris, the Prime Minister was known to support ideas for Algerian independence and a cease-fire in the war. General Massu in Algiers replied by telling a huge crowd in Algiers that the army would 'fight on'—if necessary against the Paris government. In this dangerous situation France turned again to de Gaulle.

2 Write out a list of reasons to explain why the Algerian Arabs wanted total independence from France. Write a second list to explain why France wanted to hang on to Algeria.

French paratroops parade in Paris before going to Algeria, 1957

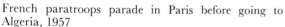

The 5th Republic

 'Can anyone believe that at sixty-seven years of age, I am going to be a dictator?'

de Gaulle, 1958

On 15 May 1958, General de Gaulle, who had been living in retirement for 12 years announced, 'I am ready to return.' The rebels said he would keep Algeria for France; the communists and socialists thought that France needed a 'strong man' for a short time.

De Gaulle demanded total power for two years 'to save France from civil war.' The National Assembly voted him full powers and the President resigned to allow de Gaulle to become head of the government. It was a revolution without bloodshed. The 4th Republic collapsed and it was decided that France should have a completely new form of government.

One of the first things de Gaulle did was to fly to Algiers. When he stood on a balcony, a huge sea of faces shouted their welcome. The army generals thought that de Gaulle would continue to fight the FLN. But he wanted to end the war quickly. He asked Ben Bella and the Arabs to choose either complete independence from France or self-government with a lot of French aid. The nationalists wanted independence. Four of the French army generals chose to fight on. They plotted against de Gaulle, were arrested by him, and were given long terms of imprisonment.

The 'Algerian problem' now entered its last phase. The 'die-hard' Europeans formed a Secret Army Organization (the OAS) and made a last desperate attempt to hold Algeria. Bombs were thrown into offices and shops. When French soldiers were killed, fighting flared up in Algeria. There were attempts to kill de Gaulle. In 1961 a bomb exploded when his car went over it. In 1962 a gang ambushed him. A hundred bullets hit his car but de Gaulle and his wife were unharmed. 'Those gentlemen are poor shots,' he said.

In July 1962, Algeria became independent. De Gaulle had brought peace but at a great cost. He had thousands of enemies, many of them French-Algerians who left their homes and jobs to live in France. And again, as in 1945, France needed to recover from a period of chaos.

France in peril. This cartoon is from a Russian newspaper. After de Gaulle gave Algeria its independence, it looked for a time as if the generals in the French Army (on the right), leading the famous paratroops, would take over all of France (the lady in the cartoon). Look at the parachute: what is the symbol on it? What does this tell you about what the Russians thought of the generals?

3 Draw or trace an outline map of France and Algeria. On your map, mark in Paris, Marseilles (the port on the Mediterranean Sea), Algiers. Find out where the oil wells are situated in Algeria and draw a line on your map to show the pipeline's route to the coast. Shade in the mountains where the FLN hid.
4 Draw a cartoon to show de Gaulle's take-over of power in 1958.

De Gaulle and After

Under the leadership of President de Gaulle, France now became a much more stable and prosperous country. France and West Germany had taken over the leadership of the Common Market (EEC) which had been formed in 1957. When Britain applied to join the Market, the French President refused to allow it. He thought that Britain was too close to the USA and Commonwealth countries, and he did not want a rival within the EEC. De Gaulle was successful in working with Chancellor Adenauer of West Germany, and by burying the past in this way, de Gaulle showed that he was a great statesman.

The constitution of the 5th Republic gave the President and the ministers (whom he appointed) considerable powers. In the first six months, over 300 new laws were put into effect to improve France's financial and industrial position.

Abroad, de Gaulle insisted that France should be seen as a world power. He invited Khrushchev of the USSR to Paris. Three different Presidents of the USA visited him to try to improve relations with America. De Gaulle made France a power to be reckoned with in the EEC, NATO and the United Nations. He equipped the army with nuclear weapons. At the same time, he realized that France could no longer hang on to her colonies. He worked out a scheme called 'the French Community'—a kind of union led by France—for the African territories, but this didn't work because the black Africans wanted to be entirely free of France. In Algeria, independence was given in 1962.

The Student Revolutions, 1968

By 1968, de Gaulle had given France 10 years of peace and recovery. But there was much criticism of his conservative policies. In May 1968, students and workers took to the streets to shout for reforms. De Gaulle weathered the storm and police and troops took down the barricades that students had erected in Paris. But in November 1968 there was a financial crisis. De Gaulle suddenly announced a wage freeze and cuts in government spending. Students roamed through the streets in protest.

In April 1969, in a referendum (a vote by everyone for or against something) de Gaulle won only 48 per cent of the votes. He immediately resigned and a year later died in retirement.

Since then, France has continued to make good economic progress. New leaders were prepared to make educational reforms and to allow Britain and others to join the Common Market. In the 1970s, France enjoyed a period of economic success based on the reforms and policies of President de Gaulle in the 1960s.

---

5 Write out a list of the achievements of President de Gaulle and his government between 1958 and 1968.

Students at the barricades in Paris, May 1968

5 Two New Germanies

In March 1945, Dr Konrad Adenauer, who had been imprisoned for a time in a Nazi concentration camp, was asked by the American forces to become Lord Mayor of Cologne, a city almost totally destroyed by Allied bombing. As in other parts of Germany, old and young people had been set to work to clear the rubble from the streets and begin the work of rebuilding shattered Germany. After six months, Adenauer was accused by the British commander of the area of being too slow. He was dismissed and turned his attention, at the age of 70, to national politics.

While this was happening, the Allies were deciding the fate of Germany. Leading Nazis were put on trial at Nuremberg. Goering and others were sentenced to death. In Poland, Czechoslovakia and other parts of Europe which had suffered from German cruelty, Nazis were hanged at the scene of their crimes. Among them was Rudolf Höss, commandant of Auschwitz concentration camp where thousands of Jews had been gassed to death.

In 1945, the USSR, USA, Britain and France divided Germany into four zones, after a large slice of eastern Germany had been transferred to Poland. These zones were administered by the four powers and their armies. The Russians immediately dismantled factories and the machinery in them, and carried everything away into the USSR. Goods from any German industry that was still in production were also taken off. Stalin intended to keep Germany weak for many years to come.

In western Germany, the Allies hoped that the Germans would eventually be able to

The end of the Third Reich. On 8 May 1945, Russian soldiers placed the red flag on the roof of the Reichstag, Berlin's parliament building. Nearby, in a bunker, soldiers found the burned body of Hitler.

support themselves. But in the meantime, American aid poured in to feed and clothe the people who had survived the war.

The Federal Republic

The Allies wanted the Germans to stand on their own feet as soon as possible. In 1948 it was decided to set up a West German state, made up from the three western zones. The new Germany was to be called the Federal Republic. It would be independent but would not have an army. In 1949 the Federal Republic came into being.

---

1 Make a list of the problems that faced the German people and the Allied occupying forces in the period 1945–9.

Berlin

The Russians were furious with the Allies. In turn, they set up (in October 1949) a separate state in the east called the German Democratic Republic (or DDR). Over 61 million people lived in West Germany, to 16 million in the East. Berlin was also divided: the three Allied zones became West Berlin: East Berlin was part of communist DDR.

In June 1948 the Russians stopped all road and rail links between West Germany and West Berlin. By round-the-clock flights, the British and Americans were able to fly supplies into West Berlin (*see page 12*) until the Russians reopened the roads in May 1949.

The Work of Recovery

Dr Adenauer, the leader of the main party, the Christian Democrats, became Chancellor in 1949. He led the amazing recovery that West Germany made in the 1950s. The Americans continued to pour in money. This was used to rebuild factories, re-open mines and begin production. Cheap loans to house buyers meant that there was a boom in the building industry. Out of the blackened ruins of the cities arose a new Germany. In 1950 West Germany's loss on trade was 364 million marks. In 1956, after only six years, the trade surplus, or profit, was 485 million marks. The Germans worked frantically hard. They achieved what has been called 'the economic miracle'. In the 1960s, the success story continued, for West Germany became one of the leading nations in the Common Market or European Economic Community, formed in 1957.

Dr Adenauer, wise and firm, masterminded this recovery. His party won elections, although in 1961 he had to form a coalition with another party to stay as Chancellor. Finally, in 1963, at the age of 87, he retired. He was succeeded by Dr Ludwig Erhard, who had been responsible for economic policy in the years of the 'miracle'. In 1966 he resigned and since then West Germany has had several Chancellors, capable men but none of them as outstanding as *Der Alte*, as the Germans called Adenauer, 'the Old One'.

Dr Adenauer speaking in the West German Parliament

 Our whole effort will be to direct as many minds and hands as possible to the production of consumer goods.'
Dr Adenauer, 1949

2 The picture of West Berlin shows the ruins of the Kaiser Wilhelm Church, burned during the war.
Make a list of other things in the picture which show evidence of West Germany's 'economic miracle' and recovery.
What goods can you think of (Mercedes-Benz cars, for instance) that are produced in West Germany?

West Berlin 1970

East Germany

In the first 10 years after 1945, the USSR emptied eastern Europe. Khrushchev later agreed that the Soviet Union had taken goods valued at £250 million from East Germany in the form of machinery, raw materials and even railway tracks. The Communist Party, which was under the control of Moscow, copied the Five-Year Plans of the USSR. On the land, farms were broken up and given to peasant workers. Then, in the 1950s, the order was given to form collectives, with groups of farms owned and worked by a team. This policy was not popular, and it did not at first lead to a big increase in food production.

The years up to 1958 were very hard. Food was scarce, shops had few goods to sell, prices were high and wages low. Ruling over East Germany was Walter Ulbricht, boss of the Communist Party, trained in Russia, tough and no-nonsense in his attitude to those who did not agree with him. He ruled until 1971 when he was forced to resign at the age of 77. Like Stalin's, the face of Ulbricht appeared everywhere on posters and in newspapers 'His framed picture is in every office, clubhouse and factory bulletin board in the country. Chemical plants, pig-farms and trawler fleets are named after him', wrote a visitor.

When Stalin died in 1953, there was a rising by workers in East Berlin. But Soviet troops soon restored order. In 1956 the unrest spread to Poland and Hungary and the Russians, with Khrushchev instead of Stalin giving a lead, decided that eastern Europe should be allowed more freedom. By 1971 Ulbricht had gone and new men were in control in East Germany. Erich Honecker, the new Communist Party leader, was also a hard man but the young communists who were in control of East Germany's economic policy used both socialist and capitalist methods in industry. As a result, East Germany made startling economic progress in the 1960s and 1970s. East German

Young people in East Berlin give the clenched-fist salute of communism

cameras, watches, machine tools, chemical products and steel were sold abroad. The standard of living rose and by 1978 East Germany had become the richest and most successful of the nations of eastern Europe.

The pride and dedication of East Germany was seen by the rest of the world at the Munich and Montreal Olympic Games when German athletes won a large number of medals, many more than people thought could be won by a country with a population of only 16 millions.

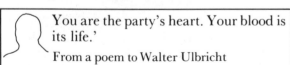

You are the party's heart. Your blood is its life.'

From a poem to Walter Ulbricht

3 Copy the beginnings of these sentences into your notebook, and add your own endings:
a) The USSR seized East German goods in 1945–9 because . . . .
. . . .
b) Changes made by the Communist Party in East Germany after 1945 were . . . .
. . . .
c) The prosperity of East Germany in the 1970s could be seen in . . . .
. . . .
. . . .

The Berlin Wall

In 1955, West Germany became a totally independent state which meant that it could have its own army. Adenauer joined the NATO alliance and accepted 100 million marks' worth of American aid in the form of planes, tanks, guns and other equipment. The USSR angrily criticized the Allies for allowing a German army to be formed. Every time there was a cartoon of Adenauer in Russian newspapers, he was seen to be holding a swastika. In turn, the Soviet Union formed the East German army and drew it into the Warsaw Pact military alliance.

As West Germany's prosperity grew, East Germans streamed across the frontier at the rate of 600 a day. The DDR was bleeding to death. When armed guards were posted, people risked their lives to escape, and some were shot dead. Not only students crossed, but also farmworkers and factory workers, and even soldiers ran away. In 1961, suddenly and without warning, the East Germans built a concrete wall around West Berlin, sealing the city off from the rest of the city. The frontiers of the Iron Curtain were also strengthened, from the Baltic Sea to the border with Austria. A strict system of passes and permits stopped people in West Berlin from visiting their families and friends who lived in the East.

When President Kennedy of the USA visited West Berlin, he told the Germans 'we are all Berliners now'. He meant that the Allies had to stand firm against Soviet power. A sign of Germany's new stature in Europe came when Adenauer and President de Gaulle signed a friendship treaty in 1963 between two peoples that had been bitter enemies in the Second World War.

In the 1970s the socialist party (SPD) came to power, first under Willy Brandt who had been Mayor of Berlin, and then under Helmut Schmidt. For a time West Germany was threatened by extremist groups who bombed and murdered. But the power and prosperity of West Germany both in Europe and in the world's trading markets went on and at the end of the 1970s it did not seem as if the 'economic miracle' had come to an end.

A wedding at the Wall, 1969. A wedding party in West Berlin wave to friends and relatives who live at the other side of the Berlin Wall, in the eastern part of the city.

4 These steps show events in West and East Germany from 1945 to 1978. Copy the chart into your notebook. Two events are missing. Add them, in the right spaces.
1945 Germany divided into four occupation zones
  1948 Berlin air-lift begins
   1949
    1953 workers' rising in East Berlin
    1955 West Germany joins NATO
     1957
      1961 Berlin Wall built
       1963 treaty signed between France and West Germany
        1969 Willy Brandt is elected Chancellor of West Germany
        1971 Walter Ulbricht retires

The missing events are:
a) West Germany signs the Treaty of Rome and enters the Common Market
b) Konrad Adenauer becomes Chancellor of West Germany.

6   Britain at Peace, 1945–56

Recovery

In the General Election of July 1945, Labour won a total of 393 seats in the House of Commons, to the Conservatives' 213. Winston Churchill, who had been Britain's war leader, resigned and Clement Attlee became Prime Minister. The Labour Government faced great problems. The most immediate was to rebuild cities shattered by bombing. At the same time, there were food and fuel shortages. Factory machinery was worn out, and there was no money to pay for new equipment.

Sir Stafford Cripps, Chancellor of the Exchequer, put into effect a policy of 'austerity'. Cripps asked people to work harder for the same wages, to accept rationing, and not to buy goods that could be exported. Imports were controlled, and tobacco, beer and other goods were heavily taxed.

In 1947 the struggle to boost exports received help from Marshall Aid, a system of financial help from the USA. Conditions in Britain slowly improved and rationing of bread and potatoes ended in 1947. A year later clothes rationing ended. The severe winter of 1947–8, when snow and ice impeded transport for months, was probably the worst time for Britain since the War had ended. Factories had to close because of the cold; there were power cuts, and people did not have enough coal to heat their homes.

Nationalization

The Labour Party had promised to take Britain's major industries into state control (nationalization). This meant that large industries would be owned by the state and run for the benefit of everyone, not just the few owners and company shareholders.

In 1946, the Bank of England was taken over, and was followed in 1947 by the coal industry, the airlines and electricity. A year later, the docks, road haulage, gas and the railways were nationalized. Finally, in 1949, the iron and steel industry was brought under state control.

Clement Attlee

Sir Stafford Cripps, Chancellor of the Exchequer (right) guides Britain through the harsh winter of 1947–8 with promises of an even tougher time ahead.

All of these huge concerns were placed under special Boards, such as the National Coal Board, the Gas Board and the Electricity Board.

The Government paid compensation to the owners of these industries, but it did not have enough money to invest on a large scale. As a result, the state industries ran up large debts in the 1950s, and were criticized for it.

In 1950, the Labour Party won the election, but its majority in the House of Commons was cut to only six seats.

The Welfare State

One of the great achievements of the post-war Labour Government was to set up the National Health Service. By extending the health and social services, and by helping the old and the unemployed, it has been said that the Labour Government laid the foundations of 'the welfare state'. This means that by paying weekly contributions, towards insurance stamps, workers and employers could obtain state help. This assistance lasted people throughout their lives—'from the cradle to the grave' as one Labour slogan put it.

Among the benefits were free treatment by a doctor or in a hospital, free medicines and maternity benefits, clinics for baby care, welfare foods for young children, and family allowances.

Nationalization: on 1 January 1947 the coal mines of Britain passed into the ownership of the National Coal Board

For working men and women, the state provided insurance to help people when they are sick or unemployed. Widows' pensions and old age pensions, and extra help for families who are very poor or in need, were also improved on. Not all of these schemes were new. What the Labour Government did was to add to them, and to provide benefits for everyone, without a 'means test' to see how much money people had before they could obtain state benefits.

The Labour Government also helped education. Following the Education Act of 1944, money was provided to build the secondary and technical schools planned for in the Act. More young people who wanted to go to university were given grants, and the school leaving age was raised to fifteen.

At last! Sweet rationing ends and queues form

1 Explain what the Labour Governments of 1945–51 did:
   a) to end rationing;
   b) to nationalize industry;
   c) to set up the welfare state;
   d) to provide educational opportunities.

Health and Housing

A Labour Party election poster

The attack on the problems of health was led by Aneurin Bevan who was Minister of Health from 1945 to 1950. His great ambition was to set up a free health service. He planned the National Health Service Act, passed in 1946. The whole range of medical treatment, from operations to medicines, was to come from taxation. All the hospitals (except teaching hospitals) were taken into state ownership under the Ministry of Health. For a time, doctors' surgeries were full of people wanting free false teeth, spectacles and other aids. Bevan pointed out that the demand came because these services had been neglected for so long. The Health Service was very costly, and it was decided to ask people to pay part of the cost of prescriptions, teeth and spectacles. Bevan resigned from the Government in 1950 in protest.

Another great problem was housing. During the war, almost a third of all British homes had been damaged or destroyed by bombing. In addition, many houses were old, and did not have baths or enough rooms for large families. There was a desperate shortage of houses. The Government therefore allowed people to move into army huts. Large aeroplane hangers were converted into temporary accommodation. Factories made pre-fabricated sections which could be bolted together on a concrete base. Thousands of these 'pre-fabs' were built throughout Britain. They were supposed to last for only five years: 20 years later families were still living happily in them. The Government also put money into Council housing. It encouraged local councils to build flats and houses, even though money, materials and skilled tradesmen were in short supply.

In 1946 the New Towns Act was passed. By it, the Government intended to build new towns some distance away from the big cities, and to attract new industries and the 'overspill' populations of London and other cities to them. The first ones were started by 1950, among them Crawley, Harlow, Stevenage, Corby and Peterlee. Since then others have been built, with some in Scotland (Livingstone and Cumbernauld).

2 Write these sentence beginnings into your book and add your own endings:
a) The National Health Service Act helped people by ....
....
b) To deal with the housing shortage, the Labour Government ....
....

Pre-fabs after the war

The Korean and Suez Wars, 1950–6

By 1951 the Labour Government was very tired. Some Ministers, who had served in both Churchill's wartime government and in Attlee's government, had been in office for ten years. In the election of 1951, the Conservative Party, led by Churchill, won and took power.

Before the election, in 1950, British troops had been sent to fight the communist forces in Korea. The change of government in 1950 made little difference to British policy. Churchill and his Foreign Secretary, Anthony Eden, wanted to support the USA and NATO. They agreed that Britain should continue to keep an army based in Germany (despite the expense). Young men had to serve up to two years on National Service in the army, navy or airforce, and this was unpopular. In 1954 it was decided that Britain should have its own hydrogen bomb, with a nuclear weapon system in support.

In 1955 Eden replaced Churchill as Prime Minister when the old man retired. Relations with the USSR seemed to improve and Eden, Khrushchev and President Eisenhower met at Geneva for talks.

However, in 1956, Britain was at war again. When President Nasser nationalized the Suez Canal in July 1956, Eden protested. British and French troops invaded the Suez Canal zone. Eden did not think the Egyptians would run the Canal efficiently, and he believed that Nasser was a trouble-maker who was endangering peace.

But the United Nations, the USA, and many British people thought Eden had made a mistake. The Allied troops were quickly withdrawn and in January 1957, Anthony Eden resigned and was replaced as Prime Minister by Harold Macmillan.

In 1954, President Nasser of Egypt (*left*) and Anthony Eden met to discuss a defence agreement

‘The House of Commons was recalled in September 1956 for an emergency debate on the Middle East situation. In his speech Eden said that the government were determined to make Nasser give back the Canal and if he couldn't be forced to do so by diplomatic or economic means, then there would have to be ‘other means’. The House leapt on those two words ‘other means’. What ‘other means’. they all shouted? Eden shilly-shallied, but it was perfectly clear from that moment that the government were going to use force against Nasser in the last resort, and that the last resort was just around the corner.’

Nigel Nicolson, Conservative MP

British troops dig in by the side of the Suez Canal, 1956

---

3 In the extract from Nigel Nicholson's account of the 'Suez Affair', what is meant by:
   a) 'make Nasser give back the Canal'
   b) 'other means'?
4 Write down *two* reasons to explain why British and French troops were sent to Suez in 1956, and *two* reasons to explain why the invasion was not a success.

7 Britain in the Sixties and Seventies

The Conservatives in Power, 1951–64

In 1957 Harold Macmillan became Prime Minister and remained in power until he resigned in 1963 because of ill-health.

At this time, in the late 1950s, Britain's economy came under pressure. German and Japanese competition offered a challenge to British exports in world markets. The new Conservative government relaxed controls on wages, and with more money to spend, the cost of imports into Britain went up.

But, for a time, few people noticed the dangers. Macmillan reduced income tax, and sparked off a wave of consumer spending on cars, refrigerators, washing machines, television sets and other goods. In 1959 Macmillan won the election on the slogan of 'you've never had it so good', meaning that the British people were more prosperous than at any time in their history.

But, in 1961, the price had to be paid. The cost of imports far exceeded exports, and abroad, foreign investors began to sell pounds for other currencies. The government imposed controls, by making it expensive to borrow money by means of hire-purchase; by increasing mortgage interest charges and by raising taxes. For a while this policy worked, and spending fell, but lack of money made it difficult to modernize industry and unemployment steadily increased. The changing policies of expansion followed by deflation were called 'stop-go'. Macmillan tried to break through the stranglehold by applying (in 1963) to join the Common Market but President de Gaulle of France said 'no'.

In the late 1950s, Harold Macmillan was nicknamed 'Supermac' by the newspapers because of his success in the 1959 election and the increasing prosperity of the British people.

When the European Economic Community was formed in 1957, British did not join because of agreements with Commonwealth countries and other European nations. In-

'Supermac'

stead, Britain joined with six other nations in the European Free Trade Association.

---

1 Explain what these phrases mean:
   a) consumer spending
   b) 'stop-go'
   c) the 'Supermac years'.

'He says he wants to join on his own terms.'
Macmillan's Common Market policy, 1957

Weapons of War

Harold Macmillan intended to show the world that Britain was not finished as an economic and military power. He helped to set up EFTA (*see page 16*) as an alternative to the Common Market. In 1962, the government decided to build a fleet of nuclear powered submarines capable of carrying weapons such as the Polaris missiles, bought from the USA.

Inside Britain, many young men and women believed that nuclear weapons should be banned. They joined together in marches and demonstrations to protest. An organization called the Campaign for Nuclear Disarmament arranged walks and rallies which converged on London. For a time these protests seemed to win public support but in the mid-1960s the CND movement faded away.

Macmillan also arranged for some of Britain's African territories to become independent. He made a speech declaring that 'the wind of change' was sweeping through Africa. Ghana obtained its independence in 1957, shortly to be followed by Nigeria, Kenya, Uganda, Malawi and Zambia. The West Indian islands moved towards independence, too. Only in Rhodesia was there no clear way forward. Both Conservative and later Labour governments insisted on black majority rule. The white Rhodesian settlers would not have this, and so Rhodesian independence was delayed. In 1965, when a Labour Government was in power, Ian Smith declared Rhodesia to be independent, despite the protests of Britain and the United Nations.

Immigration

Commonwealth citizens came to Britain in increasing numbers after 1945. At first the main group of black immigrants came from the West Indies. Then, in the 1960s, people from Pakistan and India came in larger numbers. When President Amin of Uganda persecuted Asians, many of them were given refuge in Britain.

Macmillan's government tried to deal with this problem in the Commonwealth Immigrants Act of 1962, which (along with a later Act, in 1968) made immigration dependent on family ties, or on having a job to come to.

A Polaris missile, fired from a submarine, could hit a target a hundred miles away

In 1962 the CND on the march to London in a 'Ban-the-Bomb' demonstration

31

Labour in Power Again

In 1963, Harold Macmillan became ill and resigned as Prime Minister. The Conservatives were thrown into confusion and, despite the fact that he was a member of the House of Lords, chose Lord Home as their leader and Prime Minister. He decided to give up his peerage to become Sir Alec Douglas-Home. But in the election of 1964 the Conservatives were defeated and Harold Wilson formed his first Government.

Harold Wilson

Immediately, the Labour Ministers had to deal with a £750 million deficit on the balance of payments, at a time when the government had a majority of only four seats in the Commons. In a series of desperate measures, James Callaghan, the Chancellor of the Exchequer, raised income-tax, added taxes to imports from abroad and by other tough measures tried to persuade foreign businessmen not to cause a 'run on the pound' by selling sterling to buy other currencies. However, the 'sterling crisis' did not go away, and throughout the sixties there was a long fight to 'save the pound'. The Labour government intended to plan the economy and formed the Prices and Incomes Board to control price and wage increases. There was little time for other work, but local authorities were asked to draw up schemes to put comprehensive education into effect. In 1966, Harold Wilson held an election which Labour won by 98 seats, showing that the British people supported his policies.

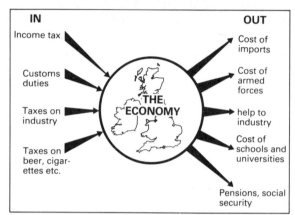

Britain's shaky economy in the 1960s and 1970s

2 Draw or trace the diagram showing the income and expenditure of Britain. To your diagram, add another 'in' (such as value added tax), and another one or two 'outs'.
3 In your book, write paragraphs about:
 a) CND
 b) Harold Macmillan
 c) the Labour government of 1964–6

Lord Home (*centre*) accepts the leadership of the Conservative party in 1963, before taking over from Macmillan as Prime Minister. Edward Heath, leader of the next Conservative government (1970–4) is on the far left.

Into the Seventies

In the summer of 1966, a long strike by seamen damaged the economy and led to heavy selling of the pound by foreign investors. Again, James Callaghan imposed harsh measures, including a total ban on wage increases. Even so, the sterling crisis grew worse and in 1967 the pound was devalued (that is, it was worth only 2.40 dollars instead of 2.80). Another blow came when Britain's second application to join the Common Market was turned down. In its remaining time, the Labour government continued to search for a better trade balance, but in the election of 1970, the Conservatives won by thirty seats, and Edward Heath formed a new government.

The Conservative Government, 1970–74

Edward Heath inherited a difficult economic situation. He did not find it easy to work with the trade unions, which after holding back for years on wages, wanted a dramatic improvement. At first, wage increases were allowed but Heath then said Britain could not afford further rises. In 1971 there was a long strike by postal workers. The government prepared the Industrial Relations Bill, which was intended to put controls on the unions. The unions replied with demonstrations and a one-day strike.

By 1972, unemployment had risen to over a million. A power crisis led to severe power cuts and the only ray of sunshine came when Heath negotiated Britain's entry to the Common Market. The struggle to protect the pound continued, but in May 1973 there was a massive protest against the government's pay and prices policy. In December, when the oil-producing countries raised prices very sharply, there was a world crisis in oil. In Britain, a 50 mph speed limit was imposed. Again, there was a quarrel with the unions. Heath imposed a three-day working week when cuts in the electricity supply paralysed industry. A strike by the coal miners threatened to bring the country to a standstill.

Faced with this desperate situation, Heath called an election early in 1974. In February the voters gave neither party a clear majority and Heath carried on for a time. In March he resigned and Harold Wilson formed a Labour government, restoring the five-day week and calling for greater efforts to get out of the crisis. In October 1974 another election gave Labour 319 seats to the Conservative total of 276. However, the nationalist parties in Scotland, Wales and Northern Ireland made a good showing and both major parties realised that they would have to give these regions a greater say in their own affairs.

Harold Wilson remained Prime Minister until April 1976 when he resigned. Then James Callaghan replaced him as leader of the Labour Party and as Prime Minister.

A major problem for both parties in the 1960s and 1970s was Northern Ireland. In 1971 troops had to be sent in to deal with disturbances caused by civil unrest and the terrorism of the IRA. In 1973 and 1978 London and other cities became targets for the terrorists.

---

4 Make a list of the main problems faced by the Conservative and Labour governments of the 1970s. What attempts were made to deal with these problems?

A British soldier in a Belfast street

8 Changes in the Way of Life

For ordinary people in Britain, the 20th century has seen enormous changes in their way of life. In the first place, there have been many ingenious technical inventions which have created new industries and more jobs. Wages have increased so that people have been able to buy more and better quality food than they could 70 or 30 years ago. As a result, they are healthier and live longer.

With extra money, people have also been able to buy luxury goods such as radios, televisions, washing-machines, cars, fashionable clothes and many other things. Millions of people can now take their holidays abroad. There are still people who are poor or homeless, and not all workers earn high wages, but compared with Britain 70 years ago, people are very prosperous indeed.

The great improvement in the standard of living came in the 20 years after 1953. The years of austerity, between 1945 and 1953, were drab and depressing. Wages rose very little. Then things changed. The increase in the number of television owners was one sign of the new prosperity. In 1951 only 15 per cent of the British people (all in the London area) could watch television. In 1954, Independent Television opened up, and by 1956, over 80 per cent of British homes had sets.

Other indications of prosperity came with car and telephone ownership, with summer holidays in Spain and other continental countries, rapid changes in fashions, and the vast amounts of money spent by young people on popular music and entertainment.

At the same time, there was still considerable poverty in Britain. Two groups of people in particular—old people and large families on low incomes—did not share in the prosperity.

Contrasts in living standards in the 1960s

1 Write out a list of reasons to explain why the standard of living improved so suddenly from 1950 onwards.

2 What are the main differences that you notice in the two pictures? Which groups of people in the 1960s do you think would suffer from rising prices?

Travel and Transport

Prosperity also meant that people could move around more than ever before. In 1939, few people could afford to own a car. Then, in the 1960s and 1970s, with higher wages, the situation suddenly changed. In 1939, there were two million vehicles on Britain's roads. In 1961, the figure was 6 million, in 1967 ten million, and in 1977 over 18 million vehicles. The production lines of the main car manufacturers, although sometimes affected by strikes, kept pace with demand, until Britain's towns and cities became clogged with traffic.

The first motorway, the M1, linking London with the Midlands and Yorkshire, was opened in the 1950s. Other motorways were added to the network in the sixties until by 1975 there were over a thousand miles of motorway. The new, fast road system meant that travel by car was quicker, and lorries could cut down the time taken between suppliers and customers. However, with the heavy traffic also came a rise in road accidents. Among methods of control over road users have been speed restrictions, severe punishments for drinking and driving, zebra crossings to help pedestrians and the compulsory testing of cars.

Another unpleasant result of traffic has been jams, delays and pollution. To control traffic in city areas, large multistorey car parks have been built, and a system of one-way roads, restricted parking and meters controlled by wardens have been installed in many cities.

As more people travelled to work by car, the number of passengers carried by rail declined. In the 1950s, British Rail began to close unprofitable lines. This meant that many country people had no rail service and depended on the bus services, which were also cut down. Another change on the railways came when steam engines gave way to diesel and electric power. Within 10 years, 19000 steam engines disappeared from the railway system.

The fastest change in travel has been the expansion of air transport. In 1949, one million people were carried by air to and from Britain. By 1966, the figure was eight million and in 1976 the total exceeded twenty million. Jet engines meant that services were faster, and in 1977 the supersonic Concorde service was

Modern transport problems

opened up to the USA and the Middle East. One of the most startling changes in people's holiday habits has been the dramatic increase in air travel to Mediterranean and other tourist areas.

3 Look carefully at the picture of the bridge across the Thames at Staines, in Middlesex. There are three different transport systems in the picture—what are they?
What do you notice about the traffic on the bridge?
What contrast do you notice between traffic on the bridge and river transport?

New Homes

One sign of greater wealth was shown by the increase in the number of people taking out a mortgage, and so hoping they would eventually own their own homes. In the 1950s, Harold Macmillan promised to reach a target of 300 000 new homes a year. Most of these were Council houses and by 1964 over three million had been built. After 1960 there was also a boom in private house-building and by 1970, 55% of families owned, or were buying, their own homes.

In the cities, the housing authorities built 'high-rise' flats. These were 10 to 20 or more storey flats, housing hundreds of people. At first, these flats seemed to be the answer to the housing problem, but in the 1970s there was so much vandalism that dissatisfaction grew among flat-dwellers. In some cities, architects and planners changed their policy, and began to build smaller, terraced blocks for Council tenants.

Another problem was the age of houses. In 1963, it was estimated that a third of all houses had been built before 1900. In cities such as Sheffield, Glasgow, London and elsewhere, the authorities cleared away slums and provided modern housing, especially for old people who were hardest hit by inflation and rising prices. Young couples, too, needed homes, but in the 1970s the high increases in house prices put new homes out of the reach of many people on low incomes.

Old People

As a result of improvements in health, there are more old people in Britain today than at any other time in history. In 1900 the average age at which people died was 46 for men and 52 for women. By 1970 this had increased to 68 for men and 75 for women. In the 1970s, over eight million people had reached the pension age, and the number is rising. Both Labour and Conservative governments have increased pension payments but, even so, many old people have to struggle to keep themselves clothed, fed and warmed. In 1970 over two million people (not all old folk) had to apply to the National Assistance for financial help.

---

4 Look at the picture below of the Sheffield flats. Write out a list of advantages of living in flats like these, and make a list of the disadvantages. Why do you think some people preferred older houses like those at the edge of the picture?

Sheffield: blocks of high and low flats were built, with paved courtyards and green areas between the shops, clubs and schools

Music and Dancing

In the 1940s and early 1950s, Ballroom dancing, made popular before the War, retained its appeal. Young people flocked to dance-halls to listen and dance to big bands. Then teenagers became enthusiastic for jive and jitterbug, energetic dances from the USA, accompanied by swing and jazz music.

In the mid-1950s, the generations went different ways. Older people preferred the songs of Bing Crosby and other crooners, and went to see the stage and film versions of popular musicals such as 'Oklahoma!', 'The King and I', and 'South Pacific'. These shows ran for months in British and American theatres. In Europe, people seemed to like their own music and shows, although with a large United States army stationed in Europe, the influence of American jazz and swing music was considerable.

Younger people went for the new American craze—rock and roll. They bought the records of Elvis Presley by the million, and danced to the loud music of Bill Haley and other bands.

In the 1960s, Britain took the lead in popular music. Groups such as The Rolling Stones and The Beatles captured the wild enthusiasm of audiences across the world. Writing their own songs, and playing them to the accompaniment of loud beat music, The Beatles made Liverpool famous, and turned themselves into millionaires. Other groups copied their style, and like The Beatles went on tours, playing to vast audiences of yelling teenagers, many of whom had travelled hundreds of miles to see them. A new dance, the twist, brought in a fresh craze, until in the 1970s, dancing to formal, recognized steps virtually disappeared, to be replaced by 'free' dancing, dependent on one's reaction to the music being played.

In the seventies, American music again became dominant. Rock groups thundered their music, although European singing groups, such as Abba, made an impact. The huge spending by young people on records, and the sales of sophisticated equipment such as hi-fi, transistor radios and cassette recorders showed that people were willing to spend freely on music for listening and dancing.

Rock and roll in a London dance hall in the 1950s

Early days: The Beatles performing at one of their first concerts

5 Write a sentence about each of these:
   a) Ballroom dancing;
   b) jive and jitterbug;
   c) the twist;
   d) rock and roll.

Fashion

For some time after the end of the Second World War, people wore drab, unattractive clothes, for like food, clothing was rationed. Then Dior, a Paris fashion-house, designed the 'New Look'—dresses and coats with long skirts and square, padded shoulders. This fashion became very popular and lasted into the 1950s when it was replaced by other styles.

In these years, too, young men and women began to set the pace. By 1955, there was more money to spend. Young people went to coffee bars, bought 'pop' music records and dressed up in bizarre styles, such as the 'Teddy' boy fashion of long jackets with padded shoulders, narrow trousers, thick-soled shoes and greased hair. The style was supposed to represent a return to Edwardian days, but it had the 1950s look about it.

In the 1960s, London replaced Paris as the leading fashion centre. Skirts were shorter, and the mini-skirt, cut several inches above the knee, became all the rage. Carnaby Street in London set the style for the fashions that were copied throughout the world, although no other country became quite as extreme as London's fashions. For young men, the 1960s saw the disappearance of the lounge suit, shirt and collar: they were replaced by more informal wear, such as sweaters and jeans, and beards became fashionable.

In the 1970s, American styles dominated the fashion scene. Jeans, jackets, skirts and other clothes were made from blue denim, becoming the new uniform for young people. The style was copied throughout Europe and in other parts of the world.

The 'New Look' clothes fashions of the late 1940s and early 1950s

Teddy boys on parade at the Mecca dance hall in London, 1954

6 By means of drawings and diagrams, show how fashions for men and women have changed since 1945.
7 Make a list of the different kinds of music that have been popular since 1945. Add a second list of the musicians, groups and singers who have dominated the music and dancing scene.

Broadcasting

During the 1940s, BBC radio broadcasts kept people informed and amused. Radio listening probably reached its peak during the Second World War, when people eagerly awaited news broadcasts and were entertained by favourites such as Tommy Handley, Vera Lynn and others. In the 1950s, as television spread to most parts of Britain, it replaced radio as the main source of evening entertainment at home. The Coronation of 1953, and the opening up of independent television accelerated the sales of receivers. Both BBC and ITV provided a mixture of information, education and entertainment. ITV was an immediate success. Advertising did not irritate people, as had first been thought, and it brought a large income to the television companies. ITV's quiz shows, western series and programmes such as Coronation Street attracted large audiences. The BBC set a high standard with sports programmes, variety shows and drama series and in 1964 secured a second channel, BBC2. In 1967 there was another sales explosion, when colour television programmes were broadcast.

Cinemas and Theatres

Television led to a fall in theatre and cinema attendance. People preferred to stay at home. As a result, many theatres closed, and cinemas were converted to supermarkets or bingo-halls. Film studios changed over to making television programmes, or made feature films on low budgets. However, in the 1970s, cinema-going enjoyed a revival, particularly with young people who wanted to go out in the evenings.

Sport

Immediately after 1945 football, Rugby League and cricket Test matches attracted huge crowds. The high point for football came in the 1948–9 season when over 41 million people attended Football League games. By 1977–8 attendances had fallen to 25 million. Television, however, brought the excitement of football, rugby, racing and sporting events into millions of homes, and, with more leisure time, people began to take more exercise. Swimming, golf, and athletics, for instance, became popular sports. Families took to hill-walking, fishing,

gardening and sailing. And, with so many car-owners, a drive into the countryside or to beaches became a very popular way of spending a summer weekend.

8 The pictures on this page show three ways in which huge audiences have been entertained. Write out a caption or description for each of the pictures.

39

9　The United Nations Organization

Beginnings

The idea of the United Nations was discussed at a meeting between President Roosevelt of the USA and Winston Churchill, British Prime Minister, in 1941. They agreed in a document called the Atlantic Charter that when the Second World War ended, people would be guaranteed certain rights. These rights would be:

- Freedom from Want
- Freedom of Religious Belief
- Freedom from Fear
- Freedom of Speech

On 26 June 1945, statesmen from 51 nations met at San Francisco in the USA. They signed the Charter of the United Nations. The aims were quite clear:

1 to save people from the scourge of war;
2 to make a safer and more peaceful world;
3 to help people suffering from hunger, disease or lack of human rights.

An American oil millionaire, John D. Rockefeller, contributed enough money to build UNO's skyscraper headquarters at Turtle Bay, New York, and the United Nations set up in business.

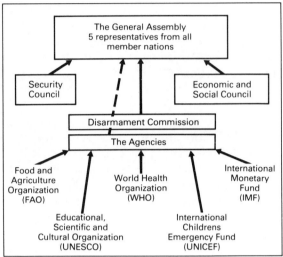

The structure of the UN

---

1 Write out a list of the main aims of the United Nations.
2 Draw a diagram to show the connections between the Councils, the agencies and the General Assembly.

Dag Hammarskjold, Secretary-General, 1953–61

The United Nations headquarters, New York

The United Nations—How does it Work?

By 1978, 149 different states had joined the United Nations. Most of the newly independent African and Asian countries joined in the 1960s and 1970s. In order to organize this large group of countries, the United Nations is arranged in different parts.

In the *General Assembly* all the 149 states are represented. When a topic, such as war in the Middle East, is discussed, decisions are reached by voting. The Assembly has to decide by a two-thirds majority whether or not to take action. The General Assembly is used as a debating chamber for big issues in world affairs. Since 1945, over a hundred different disputes have been talked over in the Assembly.

The *Secretariat* is made up of the officials who have to run the United Nations. They come from many different countries. There are lawyers, civil servants, clerks, interpreters, technical experts etc. The most senior official is the *Secretary-General*, who is chosen by the General Assembly. His office is in the headquarters, in New York. The first Secretary-General was Trygvie Lie (1946–53). The second, Dag Hammarskjold, was killed in an aircrash in Africa during the Congo crisis, in 1961. His successor, U Thant, helped to settle the Cuban missile crisis, and worked for peace in the Middle East, Angola and elsewhere. In the late 1970s, Dr Waldheim worked hard to bring peace to Cyprus, Lebanon and other trouble spots throughout the world.

The *Security Council* is a much smaller group. The main Powers are permanent members— USA, USSR, Britain, France, China. The 10 other powers (making a total of 15) are elected to the Council for a two-year term. It has the power to act quickly—by sending in UN troops as a peace-keeping force, or by calling on other member countries to apply economic sanctions (by stopping all trade).

The United Nations from 1945 to 1978

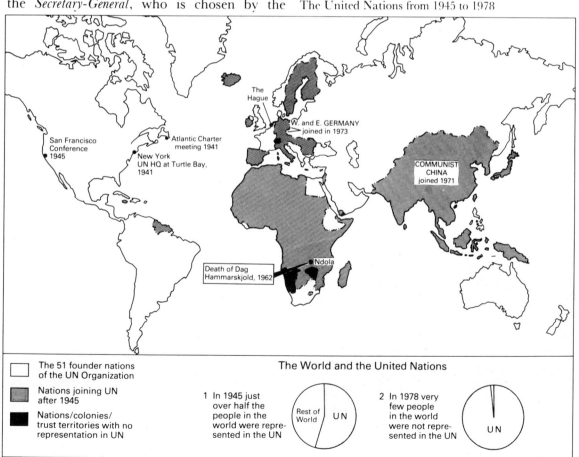

The World and the United Nations

The 51 founder nations of the UN Organization

Nations joining UN after 1945

Nations/colonies/ trust territories with no representation in UN

1 In 1945 just over half the people in the world were represented in the UN

Rest of World / UN

2 In 1978 very few people in the world were not represented in the UN

UN

United Nations Peace-keeping

When disputes break out between countries, the United Nations can step in. Sometimes, as when Britain and France attacked Egypt in 1956, they can call on the enemies to stop fighting. Since 1945, the UN has stopped the fighting in more than a dozen places. Sometimes, the UN sends observers or missions to try to work out a solution to suit the countries which are in dispute. This has happened several times in the Middle East where UN men and women have found themselves in Lebanon, Israel, Egypt and other trouble spots. In 1965, UN officials helped to stop the fighting between India and Pakistan, quarrelling over who owned Kashmir. The UN insisted that when African states moved towards independence, there should be majority rule in these countries, regardless of race or colour. As a result, UN personnel have worked in the Congo, Angola, Guinea and other states. South Africa is a member of the UN, but has been consistently condemned for its policy of apartheid or racial discrimination, and Rhodesia was heavily criticized from the early 1960s for its policies towards black people.

The UN does not have an army of its own. When it needs a UN force, the Security Council invites member countries to contribute troops to a UN Group. As a result, Norwegian, Irish, Canadian, and Mexican troops have served the UN in trouble spots such as Cyprus (where there was a war between Greeks and Turks), Sinai (after the Israeli-Egyptian war of 1973), and along the Golan Heights, where they ran the risk of being shot at by Palestinians, Syrians and Israelis.

Disarmament

Another task of the UN is to bring about disarmament. All member states of the UN have agreed to reduce their armies to a reasonable level. A *Disarmament Commission* was set up by the UN to work towards this aim. But the rivalry between the USSR and the USA has meant both nations have armies and elaborate defence systems. The UN fears that a world war may happen by accident, a war which would lead to millions of deaths. The UN has taken measures to prevent nuclear testing, and to ban chemical weapons. In 1978 the General Assembly passed a declaration which said member states should move gradually towards complete disarmament.

---

3 Make a list of the ways in which the United Nations has tried to keep peace throughout the world, and has taken action in trouble-spots.
4 Describe the structure and the work of:
  a) the General Assembly;
  b) the Security Council;
  c) the Secretary-General.

U Thant of Burma, Secretary-General, 1962–71

Irish troops serving in a UN force help to evacuate women and children from the fighting zone, Cyprus 1964

Help for the Hungry and the Poor

Perhaps the greatest problem facing the world today is to grow enough food. We know that millions of people are dying because they cannot get enough to eat. Lack of sufficient protein and vitamins leads to disease and deformities. At the same time, the world's population is increasing rapidly, and may be 8000 millions by the year 2000. The UN has been fully aware of these great problems since 1945. Aid, in the form of seeds, fertilizers, tractors and other help, has been sent to underdeveloped countries. One of the UN's agencies is FAO (the *Food and Agricultural Organization*). It has sent help to India, fought rinderpest disease in Africa, saved parts of Africa and the Middle East from plagues of locusts—and in many other ways has helped farmers to grow the food that these areas of the world need so desperately.

Another important branch of UNO is the *Economic and Social Council*. Members are elected for three years by the General Assembly and it recommends the jobs that FAO and other agencies should undertake—the control of animal diseases, aid to help refugees from a war-torn part of the world, immediate help in the form of food supplies to assist people made homeless by earthquakes, war, floods etc.

Another important agency of the UN is the *World Health Organization*. It has fought the terrible diseases that once killed millions—malaria, smallpox and many more. WHO not only brings the benefits of science to the control of disease (by means of vaccination and inoculation) but also fights animal diseases. Today, WHO scientists and doctors are waging war on modern perils, too, such as cancer and heart disease. The Money for WHO and other welfare organizations such as UNICEF (the *UN International Children's Emergency Fund*) comes from member states within the UN, and also from public subscriptions, grants, flag days and the sale of books, Christmas cards etc.

Other work done by UN agencies is the care and resettlement of refugees, the control of atomic energy for peaceful purposes, assistance to children throughout the world (through UNICEF and UNESCO) and many more activities.

> 5 Make a list of the different ways by which the United Nations has helped poor and under-developed countries throughout the world.

Members of the General Assembly about to vote on a motion

10　Stalin's Heavy Hand

The Russians came out of the Second World War with their cities in ruins and their industries smashed to pieces. And yet, although gravely weakened by the German destruction, the USSR had the most powerful army in Europe and stood second only to the USA as a world power. Stalin, the ruler and dictator of the USSR, was faced with the huge job of rebuilding Russian agriculture and industry. He hated the idea of the USA being ahead of the USSR in developing nuclear power. He told his scientists that they had to work at a furious pace to make a Russian atom bomb. They did it in 1949.

To rebuild industry, Stalin forced the Russians to make even greater efforts than they had in the 1930s. By means of a Five Year Plan, announced in 1946, the work of rebuilding roads, railways, cities, factories, iron and steel mills, electricity stations and other ruined industries began in earnest. But the recovery proved to be difficult. It took until 1952 for the USSR to reach the 1939 level of industrial production.

Eastern Europe

At the peace conferences in 1945, Stalin demanded that Germany should pay towards the terrible cost of the war and the destruction of Russian industry. Machinery from German factories was dismantled and taken to the USSR. In the liberated countries, from Albania to Poland, Stalin set up governments friendly to Russia. Soon they became entirely dependent on the USSR and in the west they were called 'satellite' states.

The high point of Stalin's policy of bringing eastern Europe under Soviet control came in 1948 with the communist take-over of Czechoslovakia. By then an 'iron curtain' divided communist Europe from the west.

Stalingrad—before and after. The top picture shows the city of Stalingrad after the battles of 1943. The lower picture shows the rebuilt city in 1974

---

1 Write brief notes about:
   a) the Five-Year Plan of 1946;
   b) 'satellite' states.
2 Write out a list of the main differences you can see at Stalingrad in 1943 and in 1974.

Stalin's Last Years, 1945–53

The heavy hand of the Soviet dictator crashed all opposition both within the USSR and in other east European states. Leading communists in Rumania, Poland, Hungary and elsewhere were 'purged'. This meant that they lost their jobs in the government or they lost their lives. Along with party leaders, there were army officers, university professors and many others who took the long road to Siberian labour camps.

By 1949 all possible opposition in the nations allied to the USSR had been crushed. From then until Stalin's death in 1953, the Cominform (the Communist Information Bureau) dictated the lines of policy. Stalin was furious about one of his satellite states which escaped. Marshal Tito's Yugoslavia refused to bow the knee. The USSR expelled Yugoslavia from the Cominform, making Tito and his people outcasts from the communist world.

A new organization called Comecon (the Council for Mutual Economic Assistance) was set up. The USSR dominated it. Hungarian wheat, Rumanian oil and east German chemicals were sold at cheap prices to the USSR. Each of the eastern European nations had to produce goods according to the USSR's needs. Trade with western Europe was very strictly controlled.

Military agreements were signed with each government and units of the Red Army and of the secret police were stationed in every country. The chains that bound eastern Europe to the Soviet Union were very strong.

Stalin died in March 1953. The men who struggled to replace him stand beside his body. From left to right (excluding the two guards nearest the coffin) they are Molotov, Voroshilov, Beria, Malenkov, Bulganin, Khruschev, Kaganovich and Mikoyan

In the USSR itself, no one dared to criticize Stalin. People were terrified of him. The 'cult of personality'—the worship of Stalin as a great war leader and the planner of the socialist revolution—reached even greater heights. Cities were named after him—Stalingrad, Stalinsk etc. School books praised him. Then, in March 1953, when everyone feared there was to be a new purge, Stalin suddenly died.

 Stalin is the genius, the leader and teacher of the Party. . . the helmsmen of the state and the captain of armies. . . his energy is truly amazing. . .'
From *Stalin: A Biography*, a Russian history book published in 1949.

Alexander Solzhenitsyn spent eight years in labour camps. In his novel, *One Day in the Life of Ivan Denisovich*, he wrote:

Two powerful searchlights swept the camp from the farthest watch-towers. The border lights, as well as those inside the camp, were on. . . . There were escort-guards all over the place . . . their tommy-guns sticking out and pointing right at your face. And there were guards with grey dogs. One dog bared its fangs as if laughing at the prisoners.

The skilly was the same every day, depending on the kind of vegetable provided that winter. Nothing but salted carrots last year. . . this year it was black cabbage. . . . The worst time was July: then they shredded nettles into the pot.'

3 In what ways did Russians show that they 'worshipped' Stalin as a great leader?

4 What, according to Solzhenitsyn, were the worst features of life in a Soviet labour camp?

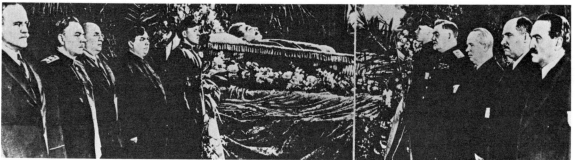

Khrushchev Comes to Power

As Stalin lay dead, the struggle to replace him began. At first, it seemed as if Malenkov would become the new leader, but Nikita Khrushchev quickly took his place as Secretary of the Communist Party, a powerful position. The man they all feared, Beria, head of the secret police, was arrested and executed. By 1956 Khrushchev had emerged as the most powerful man in the USSR, although he had many enemies. Behind his roly-poly figure and willingness to tell jokes, here was a tough man, ready to fight hard for power.

One of Khrushchev's ideas was the Virgin Lands scheme. The USSR could not produce enough wheat for her needs. Khrushchev's plan was to plough a huge area (about 90 million acres) in a region called Kazakstan. It was a gamble to grow grain here because of the dry soil and uncertain weather. Khrushchev helped the farmers who went to work on this land by cutting back on the taxes they paid, and by giving them seed, tractors and housing. His enemies said the plan would waste money that could be better spent on other things. In the years to come, the Virgin Lands scheme was only partly successful.

Khrushchev also thought the time had come to end the quarrel with Tito of Yugoslavia. In 1955 he visited Yugoslavia and apologised for the USSR's previous policies. He also visited

Marshal Tito and Mr Khrushchev meet at Belgrade, 1955

Combine harvesters on a farm that stretches to the far horizon

India, China and Britain—'to see things for himself'.

In 1956, Khrushchev made a speech at a secret session of the 20th Congress of the Communist Party. He launched into a fierce attack on Stalin and the 'cult of personality'. He listed Stalin's 'errors and crimes'. People were shocked at Khrushchev's words, although most people knew Stalin had been a dictator. Not everyone agreed with him, however, and some communists thought that there would be trouble. They were right.

 The important thing is that we should have more to eat, good goulash and schools, housing and ballet.'
Khrushchev

The Thaw

One of the first results of Khrushchev's speech was shortly seen in some Russian cities where huge statues of Stalin were toppled to the ground. A book called *The Thaw* gave its name to this period of Russian history: people felt freer then they had for 30 years.

But another result was that the people of eastern Europe now hoped to obtain more independence. In 1956 strikes broke out in Poland. Khrushchev went to Warsaw where he agreed that the Poles should be allowed more freedom. The Polish Communist Party remained in control, however, and the strikes petered out.

Rebellion in Hungary, 1956

Hungary had been restless under Russian control. The rule of Rakosi, the Prime Minister, was hated. In July 1956 students rioted in the streets of the capital, Budapest, and Rakosi resigned. The new Prime Minister, Imre Nagy, formed an all-party government and said there would be reforms. He warned that Hungary might pull out of the Warsaw Pact, the military alliance.

Khrushchev could not allow this to happen. If he did, his own life would be in peril. In November 1956, Soviet troops, artillery and tanks invaded Hungary. They entered Budapest and crushed the rebellion. The Hungarians fought bravely but were overpowered. The western nations did nothing to help the Hungarians. They feared that, if they went in to support Hungary, there might be a European war. Nagy was caught and shot. Kadar, a Hungarian communist loyal to the USSR, formed a new government. The Russian tanks remained on guard at the street corners until Hungary had settled down. Since then, the Hungarians have by more skilful means won a little more independence from the icy grip of the USSR.

A Russian tank and truck, damaged in the fighting, in a Budapest street

> News was brought back by travellers. . . that Soviet troops were pouring across the frontier. . . . During the day, the city (Budapest) was filled with crowds, looking at the debris of the street battles—a tree with bloodstains where a man had been hanged, burnt-out tanks and steel helmets from Russian dead, lying in the gutter. There were no buses or trams, only lorries carrying the Hungarian flag.'
>
> From *The Times*, 1st November 1956

5 Write brief notes on:
  a) the Virgin Lands scheme;
  b) the 20th Congress of the Communist Party of the USSR.

6 Explain what part these three men played in the Hungarian revolt:
  a) Rakosi;
  b) Nagy;
  c) Khrushchev.

11 The Cold War in the 1960s and 1970s

When John F. Kennedy became President of the USA, there were hopes that relations between the USA and the USSR would improve. In 1961 Khrushchev, the Soviet leader, met Kennedy in a 'Summit' meeting. The Russians demanded a final settlement of the frontiers of Germany which would mean the withdrawal of American troops from West Berlin. Irritated by the flood of refugees who fled from East Germany (the GDR) to the West, the Berlin Wall was built. This closed off the escape route (over three million Germans had fled to West Berlin since 1945). Kennedy went to Berlin to assure the West Germans that the USA would support them. Throughout 1961 and 1962, East and West argued about Germany and what should happen to Berlin. Then the scene of the Cold War suddenly changed to Cuba.

1 Answer these questions in your notebook:
   a) When was the Berlin Wall built?
   b) Why was it built?
   c) What obstacles were set up to prevent East Germans from escaping (you will see several of these in the picture)?

The Berlin Wall. In 1961 the East German army built a wall to seal off West Berlin from the eastern half of the city

The Cuban Crisis

For many years, Cuba had relied on the USA for help. In 1959, a rebel leader called Fidel Castro led a revolution against President Batista. It soon became clear that Castro looked to the communist world for support, and not to the USA. He seized American business companies and property on Cuba. When the USA refused to provide any more financial aid, he got money from the USSR.

In his first few months as President, Kennedy agreed to a scheme by which Cuban exiles living in the USA would invade Cuba and overthrow Castro. The men, trained and equipped by the American Central Intelligence Agency (the CIA), landed at the Bay of Pigs. They were quickly rounded up by Castro's troops and put in prison. Kennedy, who had been badly advised, was angry. Khrushchev thought him young and inexperienced and likely to collapse in a crisis. This could be the USSR's chance to extend their influence to only 90 miles from the American coast.

⬛⬛	Russian ships
○○○	American ships
◎	ranges of missiles of varying power

0   600 miles
0   1000 km

The Missiles

'It looked like a football field. . . but then we were told it was a missile site.'

Robert Kennedy, the President's brother.

In September 1962, CIA agents warned the President that the USSR was supplying Castro with weapons. On 16th October, Kennedy was told that U2 planes had photographed missile sites and nuclear bomber bases on Cuba. Many American cities would be within range of the bombers and could be destroyed in minutes. Kennedy was determined to make a stand. After eight days of discussion with his advisers, he gave the news to the world and demanded that the rocket sites should be demolished. In a television broadcast, the President said: 'This sudden decision to station strategic weapons, for the first time outside of Soviet soil is a deliberately provocative change ... which cannot be accepted by this country.'

Khrushchev answered that his only purpose had been to help Cuba. In any case, he said: 'Your rockets are stationed in Britain and Italy and are pointed at us. . . . You have surrounded our allies with military bases.'

But Kennedy was determined that the Russians should retreat. To stop any more bombers and rockets being sent to Cuba, he ordered the US fleet to set up a 'quarantine' area around Cuba, and to turn back any Soviet ships heading for the island. The Americans also published pictures showing Soviet ships carrying rockets and planes.

For several days, the world held its breath, because there was danger of a war between the USA and the USSR. If the Russian ships continued towards Cuba, the American fleet would fire on them. The President and Khrushchev talked on the telephone and exchanged messages. On 28 October, the two leaders reached an agreement. The USSR would withdraw its ships, missiles and aircraft from Cuba. The USA promised not to invade the island. Both sides did as they had agreed and the danger of war receded.

The Test Ban Treaty

In 1963 the 'hot line'—a direct telephone link— was set up between Moscow and Washington. The leaders could talk at a few minutes' notice and so perhaps avoid war and reach agreements sooner. In the same year the USA, USSR and Britain signed a Test Ban Treaty which stopped all Russian, American and British nuclear tests in the atmosphere. Although there were other disagreements between East and West in the 1960s and 1970s, they gradually moved towards a policy of *détente*. This means that they will try to reach agreements by means of talks and meetings, and so avoid wars that would kill millions of innocent people.

2 In your notebook, write the answers to these questions:
   a) Why did Khrushchev install missiles in Cuba?
   b) Why was the USA worried about the missile bases?
   c) Why did Khrushchev withdraw the Soviet weapons and planes from Cuba?

The Russian ship, *Okhotsk*, off the coast of Cuba, December 1962. Three aircraft fuselages can be seen on the deck

Czechoslovakia, 1968

When danger threatened nearer home, the USSR could still be ruthless. Brezhnev (who replaced Khrushchev as leader in 1964) had some of Stalin's steel.

In 1945 the Russian army liberated Czechoslovakia from the German occupation. In 1946 the communists won 38 per cent of the votes in the elections. By 1948 the non-communists had been squeezed out of the government and Czechoslovakia became a loyal ally of the USSR.

The Communist party seizure of power was followed by changes in farming and industry. All industries were taken over by the government and placed under workers' control, administered by government departments. For 20 years Czechoslovakia was a peaceful country, moving along lines set by the Communist party.

However, by 1968 many Czechs wanted to see changes. A new leader, Alexander Dubcek, became First Secretary of the Communist party. Son of a worker, trained in Moscow and trusted by Brezhnev, Dubcek seemed an ideal choice as a leader.

Dubcek, assisted by the President and Prime Minister of Czechoslovakia, set out immediately on a new programme. The reforms they suggested aimed at 'giving socialism a human face.' The Russians were astonished when they heard the news. Among the reforms were these:

- more freedom for newspapers to publish what they wished
- freedom to practise any religion
- the right to strike
- the right to travel abroad
- free discussions of policy in workers' councils and in parliament
- more consumer goods to be produced by industry

Friends now, enemies later. The photograph shows Brezhnev, the Russian leader (right) with Dubcek before the Soviet invasion, 1968

The Czech view of 1968

3 Read the Russian view of events in the Tass report. Make a list of the reasons that the Russians give to explain why 'assistance' was sent to Czechoslovakia. In the drawing, what change has been made to the hammer and sickle of Russian communism?

> 'Tass is authorized to state that party and government leaders of the Czechoslovak Socialist Republic have asked the Soviet Union and other allied states to render the fraternal Czechoslovak people urgent assistance, including assistance with armed forces. This request was brought about by the threat which has arisen to the socialist system, existing in Czechoslovakia, and to the statehood established by the constitution, the threat emanating from the counter-revolutionary forces which have entered into collusion with foreign forces hostile to socialism. Nobody will ever be allowed to wrest a single link from the community of socialist states.'

The Russian view. A statement from *Tass*, the official Soviet news agency, 21 August 1968

'The Russians are Marching'

The changes proposed by Dubcek and Cernik (the Czech Prime Minister) angered the USSR. It seemed to them that the Czechs were 'going soft'. If Czechoslovakia opened up more trade with the western nations, cut back on heavy industry, and possibly, like Yugoslavia, ceased to be a member of the east European defence system, the whole of the Russian position was in danger. Czechoslovakia could be a dagger aimed directly at the communist heart of eastern Europe.

On 21 August 1968, over 600 000 troops from the USSR, Poland, Hungary, East Germany and Bulgaria marched into Czechoslovakia. Most of them did not 'march' but drove across the border in lorries and tanks. The Czechs could do little. There was some shooting in Prague, but most of the opposition was non-violent. Flour bombs were thrown at Russian tanks, and swastikas were drawn on their vehicles and barracks. A secret, 'underground' newspaper told the Czechs what was happening, until the Russians found and closed it.

Dubcek and Cernik were arrested. They declared that they had never intended to be disloyal to the USSR. But Brezhnev ordered them to be taken to Moscow. After they had been questioned, they were dismissed from all their jobs in the government. Since 1968 Dubcek and other 'rebels' have been employed on manual and labouring jobs.

The new Czech government, set up by the Russians, agreed to return to 'normal'. The Dubcek reforms were abandoned. For a time the Russian troops stayed in Czechoslovakia, and in 1970 a new treaty was signed between the two countries, promising each other co-operation and assistance. The Czech people obeyed Russian orders, although there were some protests. Jan Palach, a university student, died after setting himself on fire in a Prague street.

The new Czech leader, Dr Husak, was trusted by the USSR. There were no executions, although thousands fled to the West. Since 1968, Czechoslovakia has returned to the traditional communist way of life.

---

4 Which country, according to the cartoon, is leading the attack by western 'imperialists' on Czechoslovakia?
5 Explain why, in the picture on the left, the Soviet soldiers are unwilling to kill the Czech who defies them.

Czechoslovakia, 1968. Two versions of what happened in Prague in August 1968. In the picture below, a Czech student defiantly challenges a Russian tank crew. On the right, a Russian newspaper, 'Izvestia', shows the arm of western imperialism gripped by the Soviet Union

12 The Khrushchev and Brezhnev Years, 1956–78

After the death of Stalin in 1953 the USSR made enormous advances in industry, technology, agriculture and in other ways. In this time, Nikita Khrushchev outwitted his rivals to become the effective leader of the USSR. When he was dismissed in 1964, there was another struggle for power which Leonid Brezhnev won. Over a period of 20 years, the Soviet Union was dominated by these two men.

Education and Industry

In 1917, only half of the population could read and write. By 1964, over 25 per cent of the Russian people were at school or college. The education provided was very largely technical or scientific. Young people also had to mix their education with work on farms or in factories in vacations or as a break from school.

There were big improvements in living standards although prices were high for fashionable clothes, cars, record-players etc. Most of these things were not on sale to ordinary workers. Housing was a great problem. In 1945 there were over 20 million people without a home of their own. Khrushchev insisted that money should be found to build apartment blocks in all major cities. But, 20 years later, many families lived in crowded, small flats: it proved to be very difficult to build enough flats for those who needed them.

In industry, Khrushchev continued Stalin's policies of developing heavy industry. Stalin had organized the production of coal, oil, iron and steel. Khrushchev's aims were to produce more machinery and fertilizers for the farms, and the equipment needed to develop new industries such as space technology, chemicals, electrical goods and computers.

In order to speed up industrial changes, Khrushchev set up a hundred Economic Councils in the different regions of the USSR. He hoped the local managers would get on with the job, instead of waiting for orders from Moscow. The Councils were all working on a Five-Year Plan, begun in 1955. This was replaced by another Plan in the following year. It set huge targets—three factories were to be opened every day.

A parade of troops and rockets in Red Square, Moscow

Agriculture

'The USSR must catch up with, and overtake the USA in five years.'
Mr Khrushchev, 1958

In 1958, the Soviet leaders set new targets for farming. Milk, butter, wheat, maize, meat—an all-out effort had to be made to match the USA's production of these farm goods. One of the first priorities was to get combine harvesters and other machinery on to the farms. Khrushchev gave orders for a million new tractors and half a million harvesters to be produced. The collective farms were given more freedom to decide what should be grown, and Khrushchev toured the Ukraine and other farming regions encouraging, lecturing and bullying the Russian farmers. Now that the Virgin Lands scheme was working, and wheat was being grown in Kazahkstan and other regions, he insisted that maize (for cattle fodder) and meat production should increase.

But, by 1963 the farm policies were in trouble. The prices for meat and milk were so low that they were produced at a loss. Supplies of farm produce increased by only a small amount. In 1963 the harvest was so poor that wheat had to be imported to the USSR from Canada and the USA. This disgrace helped in bringing to an end Khrushchev's leadership of the USSR in 1964.

A Russian cosmonaut

Technology

In one way, the USSR was ahead of the USA. In October 1957 the first *sputnik* was launched into space. Khrushchev was delighted that the first space rocket was a Russian one. In April 1961 Yuri Gagarin became the first man in space. He circled the world at 18000 mph and on his return he enjoyed a hero's welcome in a giant parade in Red Square. In 1968 Gagarin was killed in an air crash. Other Russian cosmonauts carried on his work of space exploration. In 1971 the USSR sent off an un-manned missile probe towards Mars and in 1978 kept a three-man team circling the earth for several weeks. The USA made great efforts to overhaul the Soviet lead and in 1969 put astronauts on the moon.

1 Make a list of the main achievements of the USSR in Khrushchev's years of power (1956–64) in these areas:
  a) farming;
  b) education;
  c) space exploration;
  d) industry.
2 Look at these figures:

Consumer goods: number of each item per thousand of the population.

	USSR 1955	USSR 1966	USA 1966
cars	2	5	398
tv sets	4	82	376
refrigerators	4	40	293

What do these figures tell us about industry in the USSR in 1955 and 1966, and compared with the USA?

Khrushchev's Problems

In the 1950s and 1960s, the benefits of Khrushchev's policies could be seen. New towns built in Siberia and other eastern regions provided work and housing for millons. The development of the oil, natural gas and electricity industries brought power to Russian industry and light and heat into millions of homes. There were more cars, radio and television sets, washing machines and other consumer goods available—although still at high prices. There were, however, often breakdowns in supplies, and Khrushchev toured Russia on inspections, bullying officials who failed to please him.

For a time, too, relations with the USA and the other western nations improved. The USSR, now armed with atomic and hydrogen bombs, reduced its armed forces by 1960 to 2½ million men. In 1959 Khrushchev went to America. The day before he left the USSR, Khrushchev announced a Russian rocket had been launched to the moon. This was a great triumph—ahead of the Americans—and when Khrushchev met President Eisenhower, he was in a good mood. The President agreed to visit the USSR in the following year.

In May 1960 a meeting of the world leaders was planned to take place at Paris. Two weeks before, the Russians shot down a high-flying U2 plane which had been photographing the USSR. The pilot, Gary Powers, later admitted at his trial that he had been spying for the USA. Khrushchev refused to attend the Paris meeting unless Eisenhower apologised. The President refused and relations worsened between them.

Another problem for Khrushchev was the quarrel with China. In the first place, the Chinese thought the Russian policy of negotiating with the USA was wrong. The Chinese hated the American support of Chiang Kai-shek (see *Chapter 18*) and of South Vietnam. Mao Tse-tung believed, too, that the USSR should help China with industrial goods and knowledge. But the quarrel was so sharp that Khrushchev re-called Russian experts from China, and hundreds of factories were left unfinished.

In 1962 China fought India in a border war. The USSR gave arms to India and asked China to end the war. Mao Tse-tung was furious. When the USSR and the USA almost went to war over Cuba (see *Chapter 11*), China supported the Russians but again were angry when Khrushchev withdrew his missiles from Cuba. The Russian leader was accused of 'bending his knee' to the USA. By now the split between the USSR and China was very serious and some of the other Russian leaders believed that Khrushchev, in his outspoken way, had helped to deepen the quarrel between the two communist giants.

3 Write out a list of the benefits that Khrushchev brought to the USSR by his policies.
4 Explain why the Soviet Union's relations with:
   a) the USA;
   b) China;
   were poor by 1963.

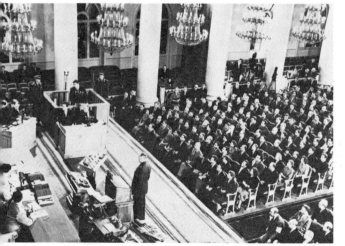

Gary Powers on trial in Moscow

The Fall of Khrushchev

By 1963 Khrushchev was in deep trouble. Many of his policies had clearly failed. The harvest in this year was poor and wheat had to be purchased from Canada. Nor could industry produce enough for Russia's needs. Khrushchev had promised that the USSR would overtake the USA in five years, but clearly he had failed here too. In space technology the USA had put men on the moon. Whenever he had a problem to solve, Khrushchev set up another department of party officials to deal with it. As a result, Soviet industry was strangled by officials and their mountains of paper. Consumer goods were scarce and expensive (in 1975 British visitors to Moscow were offered up to £50 for their jeans!)

In addition, the Soviet leaders were embarrassed by Khrushchev's behaviour and policies abroad. Once, at the United Nations, Khrushchev took off his shoe to bang the table. He was also blamed for the quarrel with China. In October 1964 he went on holiday. He was suddenly recalled to Moscow, dismissed from all his government posts, and ordered into retirement.

Kosygin and Brezhnev

From 1964, the USSR was governed more tightly than ever by the communist party. Two men, Kosygin and Brezhnev, emerged as the leaders but as time passed Leonid Brezhnev became more and more prominent. These men continued the main lines of Khrushchev's policy towards the West. Trade agreements were signed with western nations and in 1963 the USSR and the USA signed a Treaty to ban all nuclear tests in the atmosphere. In 1963 a 'hot line', a telephone link between Moscow and Washington, was installed. In the event of a world crisis, the leaders of both nations can immediately get in touch and perhaps avoid a nuclear war. But Brezhnev was also prepared to be tough with any who stepped out of line. In 1968 Russian troops invaded Czechoslovakia (*see Chapter 11*) and in the 1970s men and women (called *dissidents*) who protested against Soviet policies and asked for civil rights, were imprisoned.

5 In your notebook, write out a list of reasons to explain why Khrushchev was dismissed from office.

6 Copy or trace the map of eastern Europe into your notebook. Show the risings in these countries between 1953 and 1968. By means of arrows, show the nations that invaded Czechoslovakia in 1968 (refer to page 51).

Revolts in Eastern Europe, 1953–68

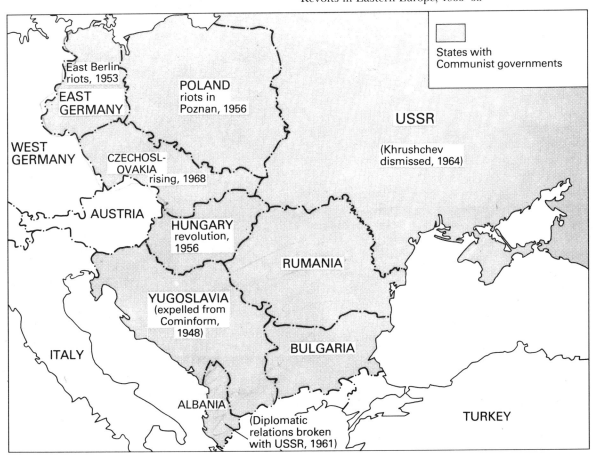

55

13 The United States of America, 1945–78

Franklin Roosevelt, President of the USA, died suddenly on 12 April 1945, four weeks before the German surrender in Europe. His successor was Harry Truman who had little experience of international affairs. One of the first things that Truman did was to support the setting up of the United Nations with its headquarters in New York. His second main task was to order the dropping of atomic bombs on Japan in order to bring the Second World War to an end.

Within a few months of the ending of the war, Europe was divided into two armed camps—the Allies and the Russians. President Truman acted quickly and with courage. The GIs (American airmen and soldiers) settled down for a long stay in western Europe.

The Cold War

During the whole of President Truman's period of office (1945–52) the greatest problem was the danger of war with the USSR. Crisis followed crisis and the world seemed to be on the edge of a third terrible war. Truman's policy was to stand firm against threats and pressure from the USSR. At first the USA held the advantage of the atomic bomb, but in 1950 the Russians announced they had the same weapon. Truman played the next card in this power game in 1952 with the explosion of a hydrogen bomb. There was what the newspapers called 'a balance of terror' hanging over the world. As long as there was a balance, it was thought that neither the USA nor the USSR would dare to attack the other side. Truman also followed a policy of 'containment'. This meant that the Soviet Union's influence should be 'contained' within the limits they had reached. Truman ordered US airforce bases to be kept in a ring around the USSR—in Norway, Britain, Turkey and Japan. The Russians thought this policy threatened war against them, and so they kept their armies at full strength in eastern Europe.

> Unless Russia is faced with an iron fist and strong language, another war is in the making'.
> President Truman, 1946

In the days of friendship, Churchill, Truman and Stalin at the Potsdam Conference, 1945

The Iron Fist

In March 1947, the USA declared in the *Truman Doctrine* that America would assist countries threatened by a communist take-over. Both Turkey and Greece appeared to be in danger. Truman asked Congress to provide these countries with economic and military aid. This was followed up by *Marshall Aid*, a programme of help which eventually totalled over twelve billion dollars for 16 countries. The aid, administered by the OEEC, led to a rapid recovery in Europe.

In 1948, Truman's iron fist was almost put to the test. The Russians blockaded Berlin, refusing to allow links by road and rail to the city. The Allies replied with an airlift of supplies, a massive operation that lasted until April 1949. By then, Truman had agreed to the USA joining the new western alliance, NATO.

1 Describe how Presidents Truman and Eisenhower dealt with the problems raised by the Cold War, from 1945 to 1960.

Truman versus MacArthur

It was when soldiers of North Korea invaded South Korea in 1950 that Truman realized the challenge from the communists had moved from Europe to Asia. After a vote in the United Nations, American troops were rushed to Korea. After three years fighting, the frontier was fixed at almost the same place as before the war. Another setback for the USA was when the Red Army of Mao Tse-tung successfully drove the Nationalists from mainland China.

The Commander-in-Chief of the US forces in the Far East was Douglas MacArthur. When Chinese troops helped the North Koreans in 1951, MacArthur demanded that the USA should bomb China. President Truman realized the terrible risk of starting a third World War. When MacArthur criticized Truman in public, he was dismissed. Truman acted with courage, for MacArthur's fame, as the commander of American forces in the Second World War, was immense.

It is my own personal opinon that the greatest political mistake we made in a hundred years in the Pacific was in allowing the Communists to grown to power in China. . . . I believe that if you do not carry this thing to a success in the Western Pacific, that it is the beginning of the downfall of Europe. . . .'

General MacArthur

I deeply regret that it becomes my duty as President and Commander-in-Chief of the US military forces to replace you as Supreme Commander. . . . You will turn over your commands at once.'

Truman to MacArthur, 11 April 1951

McCarthy and the Fear of Communism

The Korean War was a blow to the American people. A US army was defeated and forced to retreat. Communism seemed to many people to be threat to the safety of the USA. President Truman was accused of being 'soft' towards communism. His opponents demanded that all communist sympathizers should be rooted out in America. Perhaps, it was said, there might be spies and traitors hidden within the American government, weakening the USA's effort against worldwide communism.

Senator McCarthy took advantage of this fear to lead a campaign of persecution against anyone suspected of left-wing ideas. Suddenly, in 1950, the USA was startled to hear that a senior official in the US foreign service had been accused of passing secret information to the USSR. At the same time, Klaus Fuchs, a British scientist, was found guilty of passing atomic secrets to the Russians.

During 1950, Senator McCarthy made full use of his position as Chairman of a Senate Committee to summon all kinds of people— civil servants, teachers, university lecturers, trade unionists and even film stars—to answer charges of disloyalty to the USA. America listened intently as the 'witch-hunt' spread. Men were branded because they had flirted with left-wing ideas in the 1930s.

2 In your notebook, explain what was meant in the USA by 'McCarthyism'.

Senator McCarthy found newspapermen were eager to print his accusations

Eisenhower and Dulles

After 20 years of Democratic Presidents, Dwight Eisenhower, a Republican, became President in 1953. Very popular, the former Supreme Commander of the US forces in Europe and of NATO, Eisenhower had modesty and charm. He easily won his two elections, and was President for eight years. But 'Ike' as he was affectionately called, did not, after all, make much impression. In the first place he left much of the work of foreign policy to John Foster Dulles, the strong man of the Cabinet. Eisenhower, very ill three times in eight years, spent a lot of time on his farm or on the golf course. Secondly, the Democrats controlled Congress and Eisenhower found it very difficult to get laws passed.

Nor did Eisenhower handle his own men firmly. Senator McCarthy continued to win a lot of support for his witch-hunts. In the end, McCarthy destroyed himself. In 1954 he got into a quarrel with the Army. The 'hearings' in front of a Committee were televised. McCarthy was shown up to be a bullying, sneering and dangerous man. He was condemned by the US Senate, and gradually faded out of politics.

The Government of the USA

The President and Vice-President are elected every four years by popular vote. (The voters choose members of an Electoral College, but this is a formality.) The United States Congress

Eisenhower senses victory in the Presidential election of 1952

is divided into two houses, also elected by the people. Each state has its own Congress and Governor. The Supreme Court of nine judges is the final court of appeal.

The Cold War—Part 3

The rivalry between the USA and the USSR, which had begun in Europe and spread to the Far East, continued in space. The Russians were the first to send a sputnik into orbit, to send a rocket to the moon, and to put the first man in space. The Americans were not far behind. Eisenhower decided on a vast spending programme on science and education. Dulles, the Secretary of State, tightened up defences in other parts of the world by forming SEATO, a Far East alliance (in 1954) and CENTO, a similar alliance in the Middle East (1955). During the late 1950s, the Cold War 'thawed' a little, and in 1959 Nikita Khrushchev visited the USA. Another summit meeting of world leaders was planned for 1960 but this was ruined when the USSR shot down a U2 spy plane over the Soviet Union.

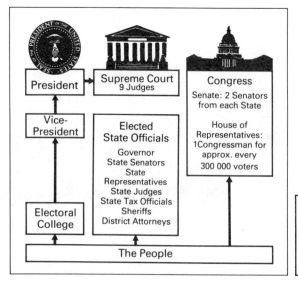

---

3 Draw a diagram to show how the USA is governed. Make a list of the duties and powers of:
a) the President;
b) Congress;
c) the Supreme Court.

The Dream of Martin Luther King

I say to you today even though we face the difficulties of today and tomorrow, I still have a dream. It is a dream that is deeply rooted in the American dream. I have a dream that one day this nation will rise up, live out the true meaning of its creed: We hold these truths to be self-evident, that all men are created equal.'

Martin Luther King,
Washington, August 28, 1963

The Negro Problem

The civil rights movement in the USA tried to bring about better conditions of life for the 2 million American negroes. There has always been a 'negro problem', ever since slaves were shipped from Africa to the USA in the 17th century. After 1950 the demand grew for civil rights—for equality with whites, for an end to separate schools for white and black children, separate places in buses, restaurants etc. The negroes wanted to be equal partners with other Americans—they did not wish to be second-class citizens. They had the right to vote in elections, but in the South they were often too frightened to vote. They were also prevented in some states from living in white housing areas.

One of the negro leaders was Martin Luther King. He campaigned for peaceful change. Other negro leaders thought that people would only alter their ways if the negroes took to violence on the streets. King won much support for his ideas. He led peaceful marches into areas of the South where he was often in personal danger. He worked as a Baptist minister, and he was increasingly supported by white people, especially students. On the other hand, groups such as the Black Muslims said that there should be a separate negro state within the USA.

Civil Rights

In 1954 the Supreme Court decided that segregation (the separation of whites from blacks in separate schools and in public places) was against the law. In 1957 President Eisenhower sent troops to Little Rock in Arkansas to force the Governor to allow black children to enter a white school. In 1961 'Freedom Riders', white and black students, boarded 'whites only' buses in the South. There was opposition to civil rights from many southern whites and for a time the Klu Klux Klan used every means, including murder, to prevent negroes from voting or joining white schools.

When President Kennedy became President in 1961, many negroes thought progress would be quicker. He brought negroes into his government, and created an Equal Employment Opportunity committee to give work to negroes on equal terms with whites. But he failed to get a Civil Rights law through Congress, because of the opposition of members of his own party, Democrats from the southern states.

When Lyndon Johnson became President on the death of Kennedy, he was more successful, and the Civil Rights Act became law. This gave blacks full voting rights and forbade discrimination because of colour.

Unrest continued, however, and there were race riots in 1968. At the height of the troubles, in April 1968, Martin Luther King was shot dead by a sniper.

4 What attempts were made to improve the rights and conditions for negroes by:
a) Eisenhower
b) Kennedy
c) Johnson?

Women travel in a special bus to hear Muhammad, leader of the Black Muslims, a group opposed to the integration of the black and white people

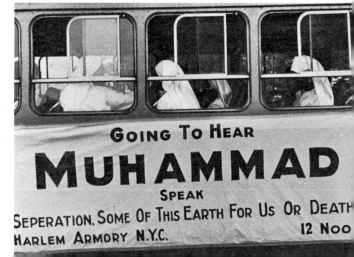

GOING TO HEAR
MUHAMMAD
SPEAK
SEPERATION. SOME OF THIS EARTH FOR US OR DEATH
HARLEM ARMORY N.Y.C.   12 NOO

Kennedy and Johnson

6
Let every nation know, whether it wish us well or ill, that we shall pay any price, bear any burden, meet any hardship, support any friend, oppose any foe, in order to assure the survival and success of liberty. This much we pledge, and more.

Kennedy's Presidential Inaugural Address 20 January 1961

President Kennedy

On 22 November 1963, a cavalcade of cars wound its way through the city of Dallas. Shots rang out above the cheers of the huge crowd. John F. Kennedy fell back, dying, shot down by a sniper's bullets.

He was President for only two years, ten months and two days. In this time he achieved much. He faced Khrushchev over Cuba and made the USSR withdraw its missile bases. He signed a Test-Ban Treaty with the USSR, banning all tests in the atmosphere, under water and in space. He set up the Alliance for Progress and the Food for Peace programmes by which American aid was sent to Latin America.

On the other hand, there were disappointments. Kennedy had plans to help the blacks with civil rights, to improve social security benefits for the poor, and other schemes but he could not persuade Congress to pass his ideas into law. He also took the step, which had serious results later, of sending American troops into Vietnam.

The Space Race

Kennedy saw the importance of the USA's bid to close the gap on the USSR in the space race. He increased spending on rocketry, missiles and other technical developments. In February 1962 Commander John Glenn made three orbits of the earth in an Atlas missile. It had cost the USA over 1000 million dollars a year to do it, and yet a Russian, Yuri Gagarin, had been the first man in space, a year before the American success. The USSR had also been first to send a projectile to Venus. Kennedy laid the foundations of the USA's space programme but he did not live to see America catch up with the Soviet Union in the space race.

Kennedy was followed as President by Lyndon Johnson. He won the election of 1964 and carried on the struggle to improve the situation of American blacks. The Civil Rights Acts of 1964 and 1968 made race discrimination in jobs, schools and housing totally against the law. But this did nothing to improve the poverty of black people. By 1968, the USA was in the grip of another crisis. In the cities, violence was increasing. People were afraid, too, of the pollution of the air, of lakes and seas and of the cities by motor-cars, aeroplanes and industry. The race issue erupted into riots in some of the main cities, in which police and blacks fought in the streets.

President Johnson stepped up the American involvement in South Vietnam, in an effort to bring the war to an end. But the stories of American cruelty to the Vietcong 'gooks', and of the rising number of American dead, killed in action, caused an outcry. Johnson, heavily criticised for his policies in the USA and Vietnam, decided not to seek re-election. In 1969 a new President took over – Richard Nixon.

President Johnson

5 Make a list of the main achievements of a) Kennedy, and b) Johnson, in foreign policy and in the USA. What problems did they hand on to their successors?

America in the 1970s

Men on the moon

At last, in the 1970s, the USA caught up with the USSR in the space race. The great breakthrough came in July 1969. Neil Armstrong and Edwin Aldrin, stepped on to the surface of the moon and raised the American flag. Other flights followed, and the Americans perfected ways of 'docking' in space, and of using satellites for radio, television and other peaceful purposes. Probes were sent to Mars and Venus, and knowledge about the planets and about man's ability to stand up to the pressures of life in space were greatly increased.

Nixon and Watergate

Richard Nixon was elected President in 1968 on the slogan of 'Law and Order'. He successfully negotiated the American withdrawal from Vietnam and was re-elected in 1972. Two years later he was accused of knowing about the burglary of the Democratic Party headquarters in the Watergate building, and of lying to protect himself. After the scandal was laid bare by a Washington newspaper, Nixon resigned.

The new President, Gerald Ford, brought a period of calmness to American politics after the upsets of the Watergate affair. He and the next President, Jimmy Carter (elected in 1976) found themselves caught up in international quarrels that threatened world peace. Ford and Carter worked hard to settle disputes in the Middle East between Israel and the Arab states. They also tried to reach a closer understanding with Soviet and Chinese leaders, to lessen the danger of conflict across the world. In the USA, both Presidents aimed to make the office of the President less powerful. Nixon had abused his power. Ford and Carter, by governing more openly and by meeting the Press regularly, showed that the increase in the power of the President did not mean that the USA was moving towards a dictatorship.

Man on the moon

President Richard Nixon

"I cannot tell a lie—I didn't do it!"

---

6 Make a list of the achievements of the USA in the space programme, from 1945 to 1978.
7 Describe what happened in 'the Watergate scandal'. What does this cartoon tell you about what people thought of President Nixon in 1974?

14   Latin America

To the south of the USA are the 23 independent nations of 'Latin America'. Most of these were once ruled by Spain or Portugal. Spanish is the main spoken language, with Portuguese in Brazil. These are the lands where the Aztecs and the Incas once lived. Indian peoples still live in these countries, but the rulers are the descendants of the conquerors and immigrants from Europe. One of the main problems today is a fast-growing population. Over 250 million people live in central and south America, and for every person that dies, three are born. It is said that in 30 years there will be 600 million people living in these countries, and half of them will be under 20.

Revolution

Brazil, Argentina, Venezuela, Mexico and other countries won their independence in the 19th century by fighting against foreign rulers. However, almost every one of the 23 have found it difficult to find a stable form of government. Many of them have governments led by army generals who came to power as a result of soldiers moving in to take power at the point of a gun. In 1973, President Allende of Chile was shot dead in a revolution. In the Caribbean, in Cuba, Fidel Castro came to power as a result of a guerrilla war. There has been a tradition of rule by dictators who have depended on the army for their power.

American Influence

Over many years, the USA has been the main protector and customer of Latin America. The USA has always warned off other nations that hoped to interfere in the affairs of South American republics. In 1948 the USA formed the Organization of American States. By various agreements, the USA guaranteed to defend the American states against attack from outside. In addition, America has provided generous amounts of foreign aid. In 1961 President Kennedy set up the Alliance for Progress which assisted farming and industrial development. However, the Americans have not been popular in the south. The USA has been accused of 'Yankee imperialism', and of trying to guard oil and food supplies by giving dollars to non-democratic governments. When mobs go on the rampage in South America, they usually end up by burning American businesses.

Coffee Beans and Oil

The USA has been a customer for the produce of South American farms. Wool, meat, leather, coffee, sugar and tobacco are also sold to Europe. Argentina benefited in the 19th century from the invention of refrigerated ships. Frozen meat was shipped to Europe and Argentina's cattle farmers grew very rich.

South and Central America

The Poor

There is a wide gap in Latin America between the rich and poor. The fine cities of Rio de Janeiro, Buenos Aires, Caracas, Havana, Santiago and Mexico City all have crowded, dirty slums as well as palaces, skyscrapers and motorways. Millions of poor people live in 'shanty towns' (built from wooden boxes) on the edge of these cities. In Venezuela, about 90 per cent of the country's wealth comes from oil exports to the USA and elsewhere, and yet only 2 per cent of working people earn their living from oil. Over 30 per cent live on farms, scraping their livelihood from the soil.

The development of industry came late in South America. And when factories and mines did open, and gold, silver, copper and iron were mined, it was often with money from the USA and Europe. The discovery of oil transformed the economy of Venezuela (the world's third largest oil producer) but most of the other nations depend on their farms. As a result, there are few big industrial areas, and most people live in the countryside.

Presidents and Powers

Most South American states have presidential government. This means that power is held by a President who is elected by the people to serve for a fixed term of years. Sometimes the President is a dictator, depending on the army for his power. The powers of the President usually include the command of the armed forces. This means they can use force to come to or stay in power. In 1970 an election in Chile voted the socialist President Allende into power. In 1973 he was overthrown by army generals. In Latin America a poor boy can, by an army career, become a general and a President. This has happened in Peru, Bolivia and elsewhere.

Power in South America: troops appear on the streets of Buenos Aires

President Peron of Argentina and his wife Eva in 1946

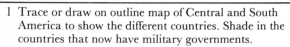

1 Trace or draw on outline map of Central and South America to show the different countries. Shade in the countries that now have military governments.
2 What influence has the USA had on Latin America? Make a list of the ways in which the USA has influenced the history of Latin America since 1945.

Argentina

Although Argentina has a population of only 25 million people, it gives a lead to much of Latin America. In 1946, President Peron took command and ruled until 1955—a very long time for a South American leader. He and his wife Eva (who became very popular with the poor) tried to help the workers of the Argentinian cities and rural regions. Wages were increased and government money was invested in industry. Peron allowed trade unions to be formed and they in turn supported him. But by 1955 the peasants and army had turned against him, especially after Eva's death in 1952. Peron was overthrown, went into exile and was replaced by army generals. There were further revolutions in 1962, 1965 and 1970. Three years later, Peron returned to become President again, but he died, and in 1976 the army took over.

Brazil

Brazil, too, is a country where the army has taken control of the country. In 1964 the generals removed President Goulart, who had run up huge debts, but had also been responsible for building the new capital city of Brasilia. Since then, the generals have been in control. Brazil is dependent on exports of coffee, bananas, beans, maize, cotton and sugar. But industry is expanding, and by the year 2000, it may be one of the world's great powers. Brazil, too, is building a mixed racial society—unlike Argentina where the objective is a pure white race, or Mexico where the Indian way of life is being conserved. The South American republics, too, are very proud of recent sporting victories, especially at football, where Brazil and Argentina have both won the World Cup on several occasions.

LEAL INTERPRETE DE LOS "DESCAMISADOS"

Eva Peron

The new city of Brasilia

A shanty town at Lima, Peru

Cuba

In the 1950s, Cuba was one of the richest countries in Latin America. In the capital, Havana, there were shops, luxury hotels and casinos that attracted visitors from the USA and elsewhere. But the peasants in the country-side lived in poverty. Over six million of them worked for only 12 weeks a year on the sugar plantations; after that they had no job. American firms controlled over half the sugar crop. In 1952, Batista (who had been a sergeant in the Cuban army) seized power and ruled as a dictator.

In 1956, Fidel Castro, with only 20 men, began a war against Batista. With bombs and shootings, the guerrillas harassed the government. Che Guevara and a small band of men, operating from secret hideouts, attacked the government forces before disappearing again into the mountains. The USA stopped supplies of arms to Batista and instead switched them to Castro. In 1958 Batista's army began a major attack on the rebels. The offensive failed, and where Casto's forces were in control, they took farms from their owners and handed them to the peasants. This won Castro a lot of support and in January 1959, Batista fled from Cuba.

The Cuban rebellion was one of the first in Latin America not to have been led by an army general. Castro went on to set up a socialist state based on Marxist ideas. Industries were taken over and run for the benefit of the workers. Rents were cut, wages increased and state schemes for health, schools and industry were put into operation. Castro's government was unpopular with landowners, businessmen and the Americans, who saw the profits from sugar slipping away. Castro turned more and more to the USSR for support. The Russians bought Cuban sugar and tobacco. In return, they sent experts to advise on economic and technical development. The Russians also supplied Cuba with arms. Missile bases were built on the island. In 1962, after a row between President Kennedy and the USSR, Khrushchev agreed to dismantle the missile sites.

Fidel Castro and his government tried to spread socialist ideas and rebellion throughout Latin America. In 1965, American marines put down a rising in Dominica. Che Guevara and a handful of young men went to Bolivia to help a revolt there but they were caught and killed. Castro's and Che's ideas did not spread widely in other parts of America. However, Cuban troops have appeared in Africa, helping rebel movements in the Congo, Angola and elsewhere.

Fidel Castro (with arm outstretched) and his soldiers welcomed by the people of Havana, Cuba

---

3 In your notebook, write brief accounts of what has happened in these countries since 1945:
a) Argentina;
b) Brazil;
c) Cuba.
4 Write sentences to explain the influence that these people have had on Latin America:
a) Eva Peron;
b) Che Guevara.

15 Africa Wins Freedom

In 1945 there were only four independent countries in Africa. They were Egypt, Liberia, South Africa and Ethiopia. By 1966 there were over 30 independent states. Gradually over these 20 years the European nations withdrew from their African colonies. Sometimes the withdrawal was done quietly, without violence. At other times the retreat came only at the end of a war against rebels. There were wars in Kenya, the Congo, Algeria, and other countries, and a long and bitter struggle was fought in Rhodesia.

By the end of the 1970s, most of the African states had freed themselves from the rule of white settlers and their descendants. The exception was in southern Africa. The map on page 68 shows that independent states have been set up in some parts of southern Africa—Namibia, Botswana etc. South Africa is different: here the white government has followed a policy of separate development for the black people. Many people fear that this will lead to a race war.

After 1945
During the Second World War, African troops fought in the armies of the Allied nations. At the end of the war, many soldiers returned to their homes determined that they were not going to sit back and allow bits of Africa to be ruled by the European nations. The British and French governments also knew that changes must come. After 1945, the European nations gave aid to help build schools, hospitals, railways and roads. African students studied at French and British universities and returned as engineers, doctors and other professions. Many of these students thought that more of the profits from foreign mining companies in Rhodesia and the Congo, and from trading companies in other parts of Africa should be used for the benefit of African people. Education, they said, should be for all Africans, not just a few. Wanting more freedom, more control over their own

Emperor Haile Selassie of Ethiopia

 Teach here today and tomorrow you will be dead!'

A message written on a school blackboard by a member of the Mau-Mau, the Kenyan secret society, to an African teacher who was thought to be loyal to the British

affairs, Africans were ready in the 1940s and 1950s to protest and, if necessary, to use force to get their way.

West Africa
The first major changes came in north and west Africa. In 1946 Britain set up a new system of government in two colonies, the Gold Coast and Nigeria. Each country had a council which had African members on it. The French also set up councils in their eight colonies in West Africa. In addition, the French allowed some African members to sit in the French National Assembly in Paris.

However, the Africans were still not pleased. The councils could only advise and the Africans did not have much influence. They wanted to make decisions on policy.

1 In your notebook, make a list of the grievances that the black people of Africa had against Britain, France, Belgium and other European powers in the 1940s and 1950s.

Nkrumah and Ghana

In 1948 there was rioting against the British in the Gold Coast colony. Among the African leaders was Kwame Nkrumah, who had been educated in the USA. He was arrested and put in prison by the British. The British had expected that the leaders of the movement for West African independence would be the chiefs. Instead, the doctors, lawyers and teachers, who had studied abroad, led the rebels. In 1949 Nkrumah called for a general strike. The British gave way and agreed that a parliament should be elected. In 1951, Nkrumah (who was in jail for the second time) was elected. The British agreed to him becoming Prime Minister. Thus by gradual stages the British brought the Gold Coast towards self-government. In 1957 the country became totally independent under the name of Ghana.

At first, Ghana had a parliamentary system like that of Britain. But Nkrumah stamped out other political parties and in 1960 made himself President. Ghana's main export was cocoa. When the world price of cocoa was high, Ghana did well, and Nkrumah spent money on new buildings and foreign tours. But, as he became more and more of a dictator, the people grew restless. In 1966 when he was in China, the army generals seized power in Ghana. Nkrumah then lived in exile until he died.

Nigeria

The British also moved Nigeria slowly towards independence which came in 1960. But the three main tribes—the Hausa, Yoruba and Ibo—disliked each other. In 1966 the army took power in Nigeria. The Ibo people rebelled and fought for an independent state of Biafra. But the Ibos lost the civil war which caused great hardship and suffering.

The French Colonies in North Africa

The French also gave way to demands for independence. In 1955 Tunisia in the north was given the right of self-government, and Morocco became completely independent a year later. In Algeria, things were different. The French did not regard Algeria as a colony but as part of France. French families had settled in Algeria and did not want to leave. A bitter and cruel war was fought between the Algerian rebels (called the FLN) and the French army. Eventually, in 1962, President de Gaulle granted full independence for Algeria and the war came to an end.

Days of triumph, days of failure

The top picture shows President Nkrumah of Ghana with President Nasser of Egypt. The lower picture is when Nkrumah was overthrown and newspapermen celebrated. A soldier is standing nearby, ready to take over.

2 In your notebook, write paragraphs about:
   a) Kwame Nkrumah and Ghana;
   b) the war in Biafra;
   c) the Algerian war.

French West Africa

In the 1950s the African chiefs in French West Africa demanded councils with considerable powers. In 1958 President de Gaulle tried to win the African leaders over to the idea of the *French Community*. This was an organization led by France which the African states could join if they wished. But between 1958 and 1960 most of France's African colonies became independent states and took new names—Mali, Chad Mauretania, Dahomey, Guinea, Niger etc. These new states joined the United Nations and most of them withdrew from the French Community which (unlike the British Commonwealth) came to an end.

East Africa

Trouble also came to East Africa. White settlers who farmed in Kenya were unwilling to give way to African demands for independence. In addition, there were many Asians in Kenya and Uganda who earned their living from trade and business. The British moved slowly towards the independence of Uganda and in 1962 Dr Obote became Prime Minister of an independent Uganda. However, he was overthrown by General Amin who became a dictator, evicted

Africa in 1978

Asians from Uganda and quarrelled with neighbouring African states.

Kenya

The Kikuyu people were the largest tribe in Kenya. In the 1950s the Africans demanded that the white farmers should gradually hand over the rich farming lands known as the 'White Highlands' to the Africans. Between 1952 and 1955 the terrorist Mau-Mau movement murdered over 20 000 people (most of them were Kikuyus) loyal to white people.

The British accused Jomo Kenyatta of leading the Mau-Mau and put him in prison. But the Mau-Mau carried on the fight and created a feeling of terror throughout Kenya. Gradually, the Mau-Mau were forced into the jungle and bushlands and rounded up. But all this took time, over seven years, and this delayed independence.

In 1961 Jomo Kenyatta was released from prison and two years later, Kenya was granted independence. From then until his death in 1978, Kenya was ruled wisely by President Kenyatta, who created a country where all races could work together.

Tanganyika

The move towards independence in Tanganyika was much easier. The British set up a council and gradually extended its powers until in 1961, independence was granted. Julius Nyerere became Prime Minister and in 1964 joined up with Zanzibar to form a new state—Tanzania.

3 In your notebook, trace or copy the map of Africa to show the independent countries there.
In one colour, show the four states that were independent in 1945. With another colour, show the former British colonies (Ghana, Tanzania etc). With other colours, show the former Italian, Belgian, Portuguese and French colonies.

Central Africa

In 1945, several European nations had colonies in central Africa. The Belgians ruled in the Congo, the Portuguese owned Mozambique and Angola, and the British were in control of Nyasaland and Rhodesia.

Together the British colonies were about five times the size of Britain. Northern Rhodesia was a wealthy area: its copper mines, run by Europeans, were profitable. Nyasaland was a poor country with few whites. Southern Rhodesia, on the other hand, had over 200000 Europeans who farmed the land and mined coal, asbestos etc. The white people wanted to form a Federation or union of the three countries.

But from the start, in 1953, the Federation was unpopular with the blacks because they thought it would hand over the whole of central Africa to the rule of white settlers. There was unrest in all three areas and in 1958 Dr Banda returned from abroad to take over the leadership of the Nyasaland people. The strikes, riots and resistance continued and in 1964 the British gave way and an independent state of Malawi was set up in place of Nyasaland. In 1964 Northern Rhodesia, led by Kenneth Kaunda, became Zambia.

Rhodesia-Zimbabwe

This left Southern Rhodesia (now called Rhodesia-Zimbabwe) on its own with a white government. Rhodesia had been self-governing since 1923 but Britain had a right to intervene. In 1964 Ian Smith became Prime Minister. He was determined that Rhodesia should be completely independent but with a white, not a black, government. The British refused and so Smith went ahead on his own and in 1965 declared UDI (unilateral declaration of independence).

We can stand on our own two feet and do not have to go around the world with a begging bowl.'
Ian Smith

Rhodesia is a police state as far as Africans are concerned.'
Harold Wilson, British Prime Minister, 1967

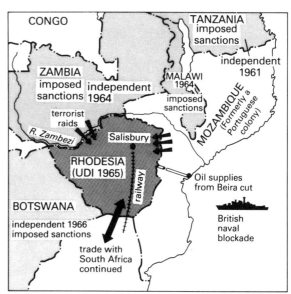

Rhodesia, 1970

The British Government wanted to see a policy which would lead to African education and a black majority in the Rhodesian parliament within a few years. When Smith refused to do this and went independent, the British Government imposed *sanctions*. This meant that British firms were not to sell oil or other goods to Rhodesia and were not to buy tobaco and other products from the Rhodesians. British ships patrolled off the port of Beira for a time, but Rhodesia continued to trade through South Africa.

During the 1970s the Rhodesians managed to keep going. In 1977 some of the African leaders joined the Smith government. But, operating from bases in Zambia and Mozambique (now independent of Portugal) terrorists fought for a free Rhodesia (which they called Zimbabwe). This led to the flight of thousands of white Rhodesians from their country. Later, in 1979, Ian Smith was replaced as Prime Minister by an African Leader, Bishop Muzorewa.

4 Draw a map to show how sanctions were applied against Rhodesia, and how they were avoided by Mr Smith's Rhodesian Government.

The Congo

The Congo had been a Belgian colony since the 19th century. Compared with other African countries, it was wealthy. It had rich copper mines in Katanga (*see map*) and also produced tin, cobalt, diamonds and uranium. The policy of Belgium had been very different to that of Britain and France. The Belgians set up technical training schools and an excellent medical and welfare system for Africans. But they did not provide higher education or expect that Africans would take over the government for many years.

When they saw other African states winning their freedom, the Congolese grew restless. Suddenly, in June 1960, Belgium agreed to the independence of the Congo. But the Africans who took over had not been educated to rule a huge country. The first Prime Minister, Patrice Lumumba, had been a Post Office clerk. In the rich southern province of Katanga, Moise Tshombe had no intention of allowing Lumumba's men to take the profits of the mines. He declared Katanga to be independent too.

A civil war began in the Congo. The soldiers in Lumumba's army mutinied because they were not paid. Belgian people who had not left the country were attacked and killed. Lumumba appealed to the United Nations for help. A force of UN soldiers restored order around Leopoldville, the capital, and moved on to fight Tshombe's troops. Lumumba was taken prisoner by the Katangan army and shot. The Secretary-General of the UN, Dr Hammarskjold went to the Congo to see the situation for himself and was killed in an air crash. In 1964 the United Nations forces left the Congo. By this time there was famine and epidemics of disease throughout the country and instead of sending troops, the United Nations sent in medical supplies and food. Gradually Tshombe took control of the whole Congo, until in a revolution the army seized power and the Congo passed into the control of army generals, as in many other African nations.

Patrice Lumumba, Prime Minister of the Congo.

5 Explain why there war a war in the Congo after independence. What part did these men play in the history of the Congo:
a) Lumumba;
b) Tshombe;
c) Dag Hammarskjold.

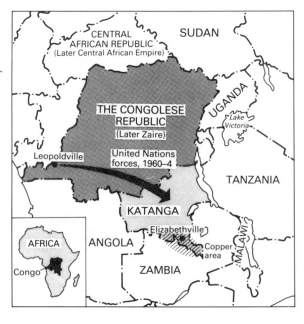

South Africa

 If you want violence, we will hit you so hard, you will never forget us.'
John Vorster, Prime Minister of South Africa, 1967

When the Dutch and British settled in South Africa, they used the Bantus and other tribespeople for unskilled work on the farms. After the Union of South Africa became independent of British rule (in 1910) the government slowly moved towards a policy of separate development for white and black people.

In 1950 the government passed a law called the Group Areas Act. This said that whites, Asians and Bantu were to live in different areas. In 1959 the government carried the policy of *apartheid* (or separate treatment of different races) a stage further. In special areas called Bantustans the black people could live together and govern themselves. But in the white areas the tribespeople had to accept restrictions on their freedom. The South African government has pointed out that the blacks are better off than in other parts of Africa. But the Bantustans are small, and over half of the black population have to seek work in white areas such as the big cities. When Britain and others protested at this policy, South Africa withdrew (in 1961) from the Commonwealth. But South Africa is respected by foreign countries because of the regular supplies of gold, without which the currencies of many countries would collapse.

Most of the rest of the world has condemned the policies of South Africa for these reasons:
- the blacks form 80 per cent of the population but have only 12 per cent of land
- the Bantustans are too small
- the blacks who work in factories and mines are paid low wages and cannot train to become skilled workers
- in cities such as Johannesburg where black labour is needed, they and their families have to live in crowded special areas
- blacks do not have the right to vote or become members of parliament

The policy of apartheid is carried further. Africans and Asians cannot buy land or rent houses in white areas. On buses, trains, theatres, beaches and other places there are separate areas for whites and non-whites. All blacks have to carry identity books and they can be arrested at a moment's notice.

In the last 20 years strict laws have been passed. By one Act, people can be kept in detention for up to 180 days without trial. The Suppression of Communism Act made it illegal to speak out against apartheid. The black people organized peaceful protests. Others, such as Nelson Mandella, set up terrorist groups but many of these people have been put in prison or executed.

March 1960: 69 Africans are killed at Sharpeville when policemen open fire on a demonstration

16　The Middle East

Since 1945 there has been constant unrest in the Middle East. The main struggle has been between the Arab nations and the Jewish state of Israel. This rivalry led to wars in 1948, 1956, 1967 and 1973. Other battles have been fought between European nations such as Britain and Arab states. A third reason for the unrest has been because of revolutions within some Arab countries (such as Egypt and Lebanon) against the rulers. In addition, the Middle East is important to the leading world powers because of the rich oil wells in Iraq and the states along the Persian Gulf.

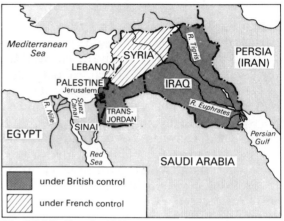

The Middle East in 1945

The British had ruled in Palestine (*see the map*) since 1917. The League of Nations in the 1920s allowed France and Britain to govern several Middle East countries as *mandates*. This meant that the League did not think these countries were ready for independence, and the European nations had to guide them towards it. In 1945 a group of Arab states joined forces in the Arab League. They intended to make a great effort to drive the British and French from the Middle East. After strikes and riots in Syria and Lebanon had led to fighting in the streets, the French withdrew from these countries. The British left Jordan and were prepared to go from Palestine but the quarrels between the Jews and the Arabs were so fierce that the British decided to stay in order to keep the two sides apart.

Jews against Arabs in Palestine

In 1917 A. J. Balfour, a British Minister, signed a document called the Balfour Declaration. This said that:

> 'the Government view with favour the establishment in Palestine of a national home for the Jewish people.'

The movement to set up a Jewish homeland in Palestine became known as *Zionism*, and many Jews fled from Europe to make a new life there.

At the same time, the League of Nations had instructed Britain to help the Arabs towards setting up their own governments. Trouble came because thousands of Jews fled from Nazi Germany and from eastern Europe during the Second World War, and they settled around Jerusalem and in other parts of Palestine. In 1947 another half a million Jewish people came by ship, rail and road to Palestine. The Arabs protested and there was some fighting between the two peoples. When the British put a stop to the Jewish immigration into Palestine, they were attacked by terrorists such as the Stern Gang and the Irgun. The British government asked the newly formed United Nations to find a solution, and said that British troops would leave Palestine by May 1948.

---

1 Draw a map of the Middle East lands. In different colours, shade in the French and British mandate territories.
2 Explain why these are important in the history of the Middle East countries:
a) the Arab League;
b) Zionism;
c) immigration into Palestine.

72

Israel and Egypt

> 'Egypt has always been a tomb for invaders.'
>
> President Nasser

The day before the British left, in May 1948, David Ben Gurion announced the independent state of Israel. The Arab states—Egypt, Jordan and Syria—refused to accept this Jewish state and invaded Israel. But the Arab armies could not defeat the Israelis and in January 1949, a truce was signed which brought the war to an end.

In the hot sunshine, on a day in August 1957, thousands of excited Egyptians struggled to touch the car, moving slowly through vast crowds, of Colonel Gamal Nasser. Overhead, MiG fighters supplied by the USSR dipped their wings in salute. The Egyptians were celebrating the arrival in Cairo of a man who in three years had risen from the ranks of the army to become Prime Minister of Egypt.

Twelve years earlier, in 1945, Egypt was ruled by King Farouk. But for 60 years before that the British had been in occupation. Farouk was very unpopular: he was often away gambling at in the casinos of Europe and he was blamed for the Egyptian failure to defeat Israel in 1948. Army officers plotted the revolution which swept him out of Egypt and into exile in 1952. Within two years, Colonel Nasser had become the leader of Egypt and he remained in power until his death in 1970.

Nasser had to face enormous problems including disease, poverty and lack of education among millions of Egyptians. He reformed Egypt's farming methods and expanded industry. His policies gradually became more socialist: industry, trade and newspapers were brought under government control.

To pay for these changes, Nasser had to rely on loans from foreign powers. He hoped that by building the Aswan Dam, the floodwaters of the river Nile would be controlled, the land irrigated and electricity supplied to large areas of Egypt. The money, he hoped, would come from the USA, Britain and France.

President Nasser

The Suez War, 1956

President Nasser considered it an insult to have British troops in Egypt. In 1954 the British occupation came to an end, except for the troops guarding the Suez Canal. The British government considered it essential to protect the Canal and the sea-route to the Far East.

Nasser had refused to join either the American or the Russian power group, but he obtained planes and weapons from the USSR and this shocked Britain. Anthony Eden, the British Prime Minister, put a halt to the loan of £20 million a year which was to pay for the building of the Aswan Dam. The USSR then stepped in and offered to provide money and engineers to help Egypt.

In July 1956, Nasser took the Suez Canal into Egyptian ownership—he 'nationalized' it. The profits from the Canal would now go to Egypt. Eden decided this could not be allowed. However, before the British and their allies the French could take any action, the Israelis declared war and invaded Sinai.

---

3 Write out a list of six reasons to explain why there was a war in the Middle East in 1956. Two reasons are given below. Add another four reasons:
  a) the rivalry since 1948 between Israel and Egypt.
  b) Britain and the USA refused to give money to build the Aswan Dam.

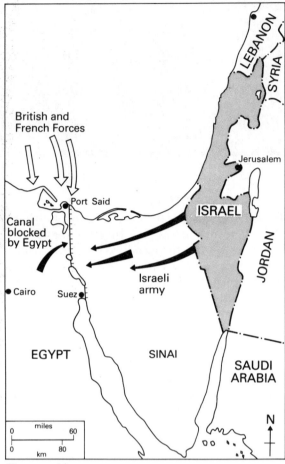

British and
French Forces

Canal
blocked
by Egypt

Port Said

Cairo

Suez

Israeli
army

EGYPT

SINAI

LEBANON

SYRIA

Jerusalem

ISRAEL

JORDAN

SAUDI
ARABIA

N

miles
0   60

0   80
km

The Suez War, 1956

President Nasser knew he could not win in a war against three powers. So he sank ships in the Suez Canal to block it, and withdrew the defeated Egyptian army from Sinai. French and British troops landed at Port Said and occupied the Canal Zone.

The Suez War was the last of the old-time imperialist wars with Britain invading another country to protect British interests. The rest of the world supported the Egyptians. In the United Nations, both the USA and the USSR spoke up in Nasser's support. Faced with hostile world opinion, the British and French troops were withdrawn, and Anthony Eden resigned from the British government.

President Nasser was now the hero of the Arab world and in 1957 he followed up his triumph by re-equipping the Egyptian army with tanks and arms from Russia. The Dam

was built, the Canal was re-opened, and Israel's soldiers were withdrawn from Sinai.

In the 1960s, Nasser strengthened his hold on the Arab world. He held regular conferences with the Arab leaders. Broadcasts from Cairo Radio were eagerly listened to from Algeria to Iraq. But, much to his annoyance, Israel had not been defeated. No peace settlement could be negotiated because the Arabs and Jews were enemies. Instead, for 10 years the United Nations forces patrolled all of Israel's frontiers to prevent more fighting.

The Six-Day War, 1967

For years Arab terrorists had attacked Israel. In April 1967 the Israelis sent planes to bomb Syrian frontier areas. President Nasser felt he must stand by his allies. He ordered United Nations troops out of Sinai, and Egyptian soldiers moved into battle positions. He then put warships into the Strait of Tiran and so prevented the Israelis from using the port of Eilath (*see the map on page 75*). .

Nasser was now very confident that Israel could be defeated. The Israelis had no allies and could be attacked from three directions by Syria, Jordan and Egypt. The Israelis did not wait to be attacked. On the morning of 5 June 1967, Israeli planes and troops moved into action. .

The Terrorist War

The Six-Day War was a brilliant success for Israel. The Egyptians were driven from Sinai

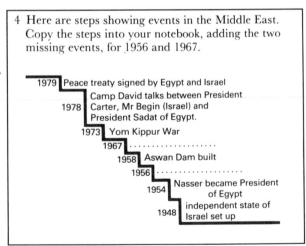

4 Here are steps showing events in the Middle East. Copy the steps into your notebook, adding the two missing events, for 1956 and 1967.

1979 | Peace treaty signed by Egypt and Israel
Camp David talks between President
1978 | Carter, Mr Begin (Israel) and
President Sadat of Egypt.
1973 | Yom Kippur War
1967 | . . . .
1958 | Aswan Dam built
1956 | . . . .
1954 | Nasser became President
of Egypt
1948 | independent state of
Israel set up

This cartoon from an Egyptian newspaper shows an Egyptian soldier and an Arab trampling on a Jew

The wreckage of a defeated Egyptian army litters the road from Gaza to Suez, June 1967

to the west bank of the Suez Canal. Territory, including the Golan Heights, was seized from Jordanian and Syrian troops. The old city of Jerusalem was added to the state of Israel. And again, the Suez Canal was blocked and remained closed for several years.

After six days, Israel agreed to a cease-fire. The USA defended Israel in the United Nations, on the grounds that the war had been fought in self-defence.

President Nasser offered to resign. After all, Egypt had suffered defeat. The Russians helped by pouring arms and equipment into Egypt to replace the supplies lost in the war, and Nasser stayed on. Between 1967 and 1973 the unrest in the Middle East continued. Guerrilla groups, including the Palestine Liberation Front, carried out terrorist raids against Israel, hijacked foreign aeroplanes and in 1972 killed Israeli athletes at the Munich Olympic Games. Israel in turn replied to the terrorist raids by attacking camps in Syria, Lebanon and Jordan.

Another problem in the Middle East arose out of the wars. Thousands of people, refugees, fled from the fighting. Many of them crossed into Egypt and Jordan. They were put into camps where they have remained—homeless, poor and a recruiting ground for the Arab terrorist organizations.

5 A month before this cartoon was drawn, President Nasser of Egypt and King Hussein of Jordan signed a military agreement. Explain why the Arabs were confident of crushing Israel. Draw a cartoon, as if for an Israeli newspaper, to celebrate the victory in the Six-Day War of 1967.

The June War, 1967

6 Draw a map of the Middle East area to show the main events of two wars, in 1956 and 1967.
By means of arrows, show the Israeli, British and French attacks in 1956.
With a different coloured pencil, show the Israeli territorial gains in the war of 1967.
7 The events in the Middle East between 1967 and 1978 have been called 'the terrorist war'. In your notebook, write out this title and explain what it means in the Middle East.

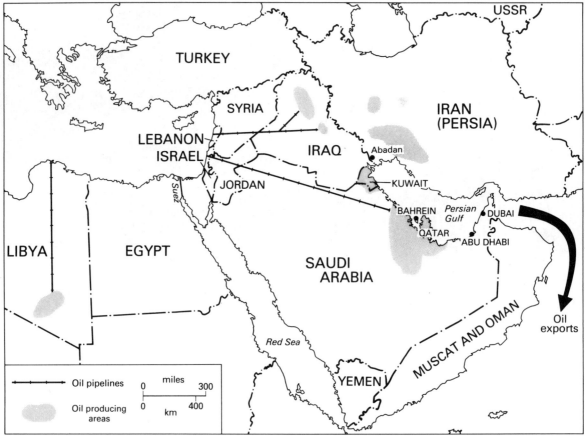

The Middle East oil states

The Arab States

After 1945 the development of the oil industry transformed the Middle East. The diagram shows the rapid expansion in oil production, and the increasing share taken by the Arab countries.

World/Arab oil production figures

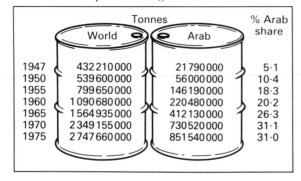

	Tonnes		% Arab share
	World	Arab	
1947	432 210 000	21 790 000	5·1
1950	539 600 000	56 000 000	10·4
1955	799 650 000	146 190 000	18·3
1960	1 090 680 000	220 480 000	20·2
1965	1 564 935 000	412 130 000	26·3
1970	2 349 155 000	730 520 000	31·1
1975	2 747 660 000	851 540 000	31·0

Saudi Arabia

One of the most powerful of the Arab states is Saudi Arabia. In 1964, after a struggle for power, King Saud was deposed and his younger brother, Feisal, became King. For many years the Saudis gave strong support to President Nasser of Egypt in his campaign for Arab nationalism. King Feisal, in the 1970s, formed a union of the Arab kings of Jordan, Saudi Arabia and Iran. These kings relied on the USA to supply them with planes and weapons and in return gave concessions on oil production.

Oil was discovered in 1938 in Saudi Arabia. Since then, the Arabian American Oil Company (ARAMCO) has controlled oil production. In 1950, 26 million tons of oil were produced: in 1973, over 200 million tons were exported. The Company devised a system of 'fifty-fifty' payments: in this way profits were divided equally between ARAMCO and the Saudi government. The money from the oil wells has been used to develop Saudi Arabia in other ways. Schools and hospitals have been built and industry expanded.

76

8 Draw a map in your notebook to show the main oil producing countries and states in the Middle East.
9 Look carefully at the diagram of oil production. By how much did the Arab share of world oil production increase between 1950 and 1975? What do you notice about the figures for 1970 and 1975?

Abadan in Iran: a view of the oil refinery

The Persian Gulf States

For many years Britain controlled the countries around the Persian Gulf. The British government signed agreements with Arab rulers who agreed not to give up territory or oil rights to any other country. In return, Britain protected the Arab rulers. The discovery of oil changed the situation. The total value of oil produced in the Persian Gulf states (Kuwait, Bahrein, Abu Dhabi, Dubai etc) rose to over £2000 million each year. It is thought that over half of the world's oil reserves lie in the sea or in lands bordering the Persian Gulf. In 1973 the Arab states which formed OPEC (the Organization of Oil Petroleum Exporting Countries) raised oil prices and this resulted in a financial and energy crisis in many European countries, including Britain. Since oil was discovered in the North Sea, the European nations have not had to rely quite so much on Arab oil supplies.

Libya

Another Arab state that has grown rich on oil is Libya which was once ruled by the Italians. King Idris took refuge in Egypt during the Second World War. After his return in 1944, he relied on American and British support in the form of aid and technical assistance: in return he allowed US and British air forces to use bases in the desert.

In 1969 King Idris abdicated and was replaced by Colonel Gaddafi. Libya became a republic, and when the oil began to flow from the desert wells, the British and American forces were asked to leave. Since then, Colonel Gaddafi has been a keen supporter of Arab nationalism.

Another War between Arabs and Israelis

After the death of President Nasser in 1970, Anwar Sadat became leader of Egypt. Feeling more confident of their strength, the Arab powers attacked Israel in 1973 in what is known as the Yom Kippur War, called after a Jewish festival.

The war lasted three weeks. The Israelis clung on to the territories that they had captured in 1967. In the years since 1973, the Israelis have continued to harass the terrorists operating from Lebanon and Iraq. In 1978 President Sadat of Egypt and Menachem Begin of Israel met several times to try to reach an agreement, but the Israelis are reluctant to give up Sinai and other lands. Meanwhile, in other Arab states there was unrest. A civil war in Lebanon ruined that country and in 1979 the Shah of Iran was overthrown and fled into exile.

10 Make a list of the main oil producing countries or states in the Middle East. What changes have the oil revenues brought to these states?

A feast given by the ruler of Dubai

77

17 Peace in the Pacific

In August 1945, two Japanese cities, Hiroshima and Nagasaki, were destroyed by atomic bombs. The Japanese then surrendered and the war in the Pacific came to an end.

American troops entered Japan and set up a Commission to administer the country. In fact, General MacArthur, the American Commander-in-Chief in the Pacific, virtually took all major decisions until he was dismissed in 1951 by President Truman.

'Number One in the World'

A popular slogan in Japan is *sekai ichi* which means 'Number One in the World'. This became the policy of the Japanese, once they had made a start with economic recovery.

The policy of the Americans in 1945 was to turn Japan into a peaceful democratic country, under the protection of the USA. The Americans introduced western ideas and reforms. These are some of them:

- Japanese women could vote in elections
- a new constitution set up a parliament
- the Emperor lost all real power
- a new school system was based on the American pattern
- land was distributed to peasant-farmers
- a new system of law was set up

One clause in the constitution said that Japan would not be allowed an army. The Americans later regretted this when they were fighting the communists in Vietnam. But it meant that the Japanese did not have to spend large sums of money on defence—unlike the western nations and the USA. Thus, by 1950, Japan was ready to challenge the rest of the world for 'Number One Place'.

'Use every minute, use every effort!'

At first, economic recovery was slow. Japan found it difficult to feed its population of 90 millions. In 1946 the countryside went in terror of gangs of hungry people who came out of the cities hunting for food.

The city of Hiroshima, Japan, before and after the atomic bomb was dropped, August 1945

But, after 1948, the situation improved. The Japanese went in for modern industrial goods. They copied, and improved on, European engineering. The first breakthrough came in the chemical, shipbuilding and engineering industries. Because wages were much lower than workers earned in Europe and the USA, and because they were prepared to work harder for more hours each day in a highly disciplined manner, the Japanese found that they could make goods at a fraction of the price of European manufactures. After 1951, when a peace treaty was signed with the USA, the pace quickened. The Japanese won the respect of the world for the quick, inventive way in which they adapted and improved on new ideas. The slogan in the Hitachi factory of 'use every minute, use every effort' was applied with great success throughout the whole of industry.

New Industries and New Ways

Japanese industry, geared to mass-production, also avoided strikes. Firms such as Sony, Hitachi, Mitsubishi and others look after their workers. They provide flats at low rents, cheap holidays and other schemes. The workers in turn are loyal to the firms that employ them. Japanese watches, cameras, motor-cyles and cars, radio and television sets, hi-fi equipment and other goods are sold throughout the world. By the end of the 1970s, Japan's trade balances were strongly in its favour.

In this way, the Japanese took to and improved on western ways. However, the constant presence of American soldiers in the streets irritated many people. In 1954 the USA exploded a H-bomb at Bikini atoll. The crew of a Japanese fishing boat caught radiation sickness. This led to student riots in Tokyo. In 1960, when a security pact was signed with the USA, there was further trouble. In the 1970s students rioted again because they objected to a new Tokyo airport. Many Japanese felt that they were copying western ways and the old way of life would be completely lost.

Australia and New Zealand

For the first time in their history, Australians and New Zealanders were in danger in 1941 from foreign attack. However, the Japanese army did not reach their shores. Instead, Australian and New Zealand forces fought beside the British and Americans in the Pacific war that ended in 1945. In 1949, Sir Robert Menzies became Prime Minister of Australia, remaining in power until 1966. In these years, the Pacific nations looked more and more towards the USA for protection and trade. As well as the SEATO pact (the South-East Asia Treaty Organization) a treaty called ANZUS was signed with the USA in 1951.

---

1 Write out a list of reasons to explain why Japan has been so successful as a trading nation since 1945.
2 Make a list of the problems that Australia and New Zealand have faced since 1945.

The Far East and the Pacific 1945–78

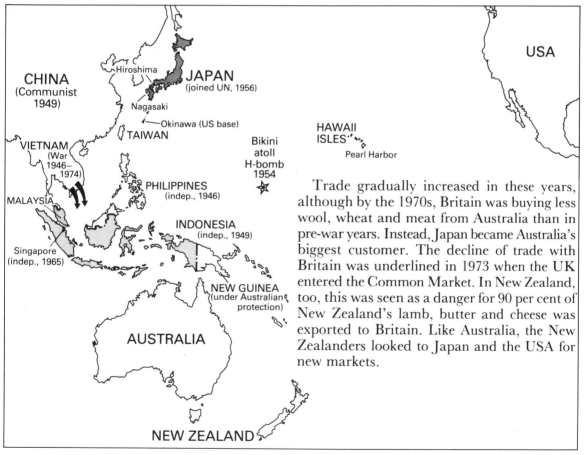

Trade gradually increased in these years, although by the 1970s, Britain was buying less wool, wheat and meat from Australia than in pre-war years. Instead, Japan became Australia's biggest customer. The decline of trade with Britain was underlined in 1973 when the UK entered the Common Market. In New Zealand, too, this was seen as a danger for 90 per cent of New Zealand's lamb, butter and cheese was exported to Britain. Like Australia, the New Zealanders looked to Japan and the USA for new markets.

18 War in Asia, 1950–54

In the 1950s the Cold War moved into Asia. The civil war in China was eventually won by the communist forces led by Mao Tse-tung. In 1949 the battered army of Chiang Kai-shek was driven to the island of Taiwan (Formosa), protected by American troops. President Truman and his advisers were by now very worried for the communists seemed poised to overrun all of Asia.

The Korean War

In 1945 Korea was divided. Russian troops occupied the northern area, down to the 38th Parallel (*see map, below left*), with American forces in the south. In the course of the next few years the Russians set up a communist government in North Korea which carried out popular land reforms. In South Korea the United Nations arranged elections, and the country became independent under President Syngman Rhee. In 1949, the US and the Russian troops left Korea. Within a year, the rivalry between the two parts of Korea had led to a full-scale war between them.

On 25 June 1950, North Korean troops invaded. The reasons for the attack are still not clear. The North Korean leader, Kim Il Sung, wanted to unite Korea under a communist

The war in Korea, 1950–53

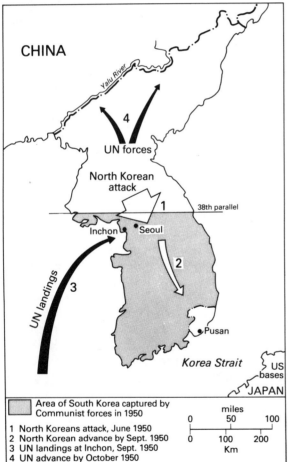

Area of South Korea captured by Communist forces in 1950

1 North Koreans attack, June 1950
2 North Korean advance by Sept. 1950
3 UN landings at Inchon, Sept. 1950
4 UN advance by October 1950

miles
0   50   100
0   100   200
Km

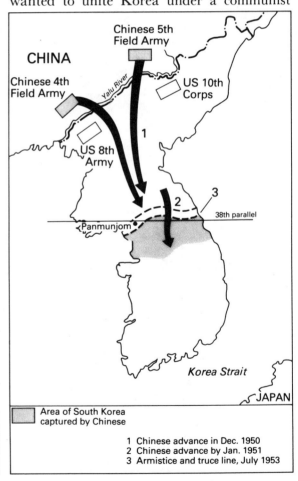

Area of South Korea captured by Chinese

1 Chinese advance in Dec. 1950
2 Chinese advance by Jan. 1951
3 Armistice and truce line, July 1953

regime. Syngman Rhee wanted to unite it under a non-communist government. Before the invasion, there had been some shooting across the border. Whether Kim Il Sung told the Russian and Chinese leaders that he intended to attack is also unknown. But President Truman certainly believed that the USSR had encouraged North Korea to invade.

As the communists swept through the South, the Americans moved into action. The US 7th Fleet patrolled the seas off China, in case the communists attacked Taiwan. Other planes and ships gave air and sea support to the South Korean army.

The UN Moves In

The North Korean advance was effective and soon all but the south-eastern corner of the country had been captured. The United Nations then called on all member states to send assistance. (The Russians failed to stop this because they had withdrawn from the UN at this time.) Although 16 nations eventually sent troops to Korea, it was largely an American army which landed at Pusan and Inchon and drove the North Koreans back across the 38th Parallel. However, instead of stopping at the frontier, the UN army advanced beyond it. Within weeks the Americans had drawn near to the Yalu River, the border with communist China. It became clear that the United Nations intended to unify Korea into a single country, ruled by a non-communist government.

China Intervenes

The Chinese had no wish to see UN troops at their frontier. In November 1950, therefore, a large Chinese army crossed the Yalu River. The tide of war now changed. The UN forces were flung back to the 38th Parallel and beyond it (*see map page 80, below right*). By January 1951 the Chinese troops had captured about a third of South Korea.

General MacArthur, the American commander-in-chief of the UN forces, argued that the USA should use all its power to defeat China—even to the extent of using the atom bomb. The Korean War at this stage became very dangerous. It could have set off another world war. Some Americans agreed with

Chinese troops in Korea

MacArthur. They wanted the USA to follow a policy of *liberation* by which countries could be set free from communist control. But President Truman disagreed. His policy was *containment*, keeping communists walled up in their own countries, but avoiding direct attacks on them. In April 1951 President Truman dismissed MacArthur from the command of the allied forces in Korea.

The war dragged on. The Chinese could put many soldiers into battle, but the UN had superior planes and weapons. In July 1953 the war ended with an armistice (truce) which fixed a new border, very near to the old 38th Parallel frontier. Since then there have been two Koreas—the communist North and the American-protected South.

1 Draw a map of Korea in your notebook, and show by arrows or other ways:
   a) the North Korean invasion of South Korea, June to September 1950;
   b) the UN counter-attack, September to November 1950;
   c) the Chinese attack in November 1950;
   d) the truce line.
2 Explain the difference between the American policy of liberation and containment.

Asia in the 1950s

In addition to fighting in Korea, the USA made other attempts to 'contain' communism in Asia. US troops stayed in Japan until a peace treaty was signed in 1951. By this, the Japanese were allowed to have their own army. American forces remained on the island of Okinawa, lying between Taiwan and Japan. The USA continued to vote against allowing China to join the United Nations (until 1971), and also built up a system of alliances. At first, the USA signed a defence agreement with Australia, New Zealand, the Philippines and Japan. In 1954, a new military alliance called SEATO (the South-East Asia Treaty Organization) pulled all the non-communist countries (plus Taiwan and South Korea) into a circle around communist China.

Indo-China

The Chinese did not stand still. The next region to come under the eye of the communists was Indo-China where a long and cruel war was fought.

Before the Second World War, France had ruled in Indo-China. This area included Laos, Cambodia and Vietnam (*see the map*). A communist leader called Ho Chi Minh fought against the Japanese from 1941 to 1945. When the war ended he announced the independence of Vietnam. But at that time the French had no intention of letting their colonies go free. In 1946, therefore, war returned to Vietnam. Three years later the communist forces of the Vietminh received military aid from China, and the French found it more and more difficult to hang on to Vietnam.

3 Draw a map to show the gradual Chinese expansion into other parts of Asia. With coloured pencils, show how the Americans extended their influence and built up alliances in Asia.
4 Read the statement above by General MacArthur. How could the Americans have prevented (if at all) the communists from taking power in China? What might have happened in Asia and in Europe if the USA had attacked China in the 1950s?

American and Chinese rivalry in Asia

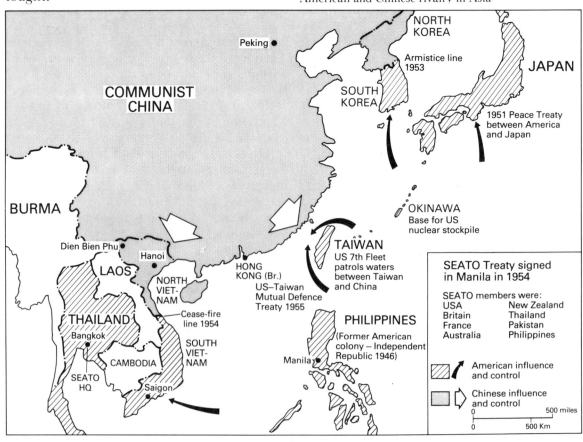

America Enters Vietnam

In the 1950s, the Americans helped the French with weapons and advisers. General Eisenhower (who succeeded Truman as President in 1952) saw the war in Vietnam as part of the struggle against communism throughout Asia. But in May 1954 a French army was surrounded and defeated at the town of Dien Bien Phu, in northern Vietnam. At a peace conference held at Geneva, France agreed to divide Vietnam into two parts— North and South. Ho Chi Minh promptly set up a communist government in North Vietnam and the Americans supported a different government in South Vietnam. At the same time, it was agreed that Laos and Cambodia should be independent and separate countries.

The struggle for Vietnam had not ended. Indeed, it had entered a new and dangerous phase. After 1954 the USA took an increasing share of the protection of South Vietnam.

Indonesia and Malaysia

Like the French in Indo-China, the Dutch in 1945 moved back into their old colonies in the East Indies. But there were by then several nationalist parties prepared to fight for independence. A civil war began which lasted until 1949 when the Nationalist Party led by Ahmed Sukharno persuaded the Dutch to accept defeat. The 3000 islands and 80 million people of the former Dutch East Indies became in 1950 the independent Republic of Indonesia.

In Malaya, when the Japanese withdrew and the British returned in 1945, the communist army took to the jungle. In a long terrorist campaign, Chin Peng, the communist leader, harassed the British and the Malays, killing planters, burning villages and then fading into the jungle. But the communists did not win over a majority of the Malay people. The British, who at one time had 50000 troops involved in the Malayan War, promised independence. The communists were gradually defeated and in 1957 Malaya became independent, with Singapore becoming a separate state two years later. In 1963, Sarawak, Brunei, Sabah, Malaya and Singapore formed the Federation of Malaysia.

Mao Tse-tung and Ho Chi Minh

5 In your notebook describe how Indonesia and Malaysia came into being after the Second World War. Add a sentence to explain the difference between British and Dutch policies towards their former colonies.

6 In your notebook, draw a map to show the Federation of Malaysia (in one colour) and Indonesia (in a different colour). Name the different parts of the Federation and of Indonesia.

19   The China of Mao Tse-tung

Mao Tse-tung, the son of a peasant, trained to be a teacher. But he never reached the classroom. In 1921 he helped to set up the Chinese Communist Party and from then he was deeply involved in its work. Ten years later, the communist Red Army, led by Mao, set off on a 6000 mile journey called the Long March. They travelled on foot, fighting for most of the way against Nationalist troops. Chiang Kai-shek, the Nationalist leader, was determined to crush the communists. From 1935 the Red Army had to fight both Chiang and the Japanese who had invaded China. In this long war, Mao won the support of the peasants who kept the Red Army alive by supplying food and shelter.

In 1945, when the Japanese had been defeated and had left China, Mao turned against Chiang. The USA tried to get the communists and the Nationalists to work together but neither side trusted the other. The communists attacked, and in a series of brilliant fighting campaigns, the Red Army steadily advanced and drove Chiang and his army out of China. The Nationalists took shelter on the island of Taiwan, protected by the United States navy. On 1 October 1949, Mao established the People's Republic of China.

Land and Industrial Reform

After 20 years of war, China in 1949 was in a very weak state. The farmers could not grow enough rice and other crops to feed a population of over 600 million people. Industry produced only half of its pre-war output. Roads, railways, bridges, factories had all been badly damaged. Food shortages led to high prices in the markets.

> 'We communists are like seeds and the people are the soil. Wherever we go, we must unite with the people, take root and blossom among them.'
> Mao Tse-tung

One of Mao's first actions was to take control of the large industrial companies and fix new prices. Within three years, the production of coal, iron, steel and cement was up to the pre-war levels. All private banks were closed. The State Bank, now the only bank in China, lent money for new industrial schemes planned by the government. Mao used soldiers to repair damaged railway lines and stations, and peasants toiled to build new roads and bridges.

Peasants building a dam: human muscles take the place of machines

'Take Root and Blossom'

One of the ways that the communists won the support of the peasants was by the Land Reform laws. These transferred land from the landlords to the peasants. For hundreds of years the landlords had ruled the villages of China, but in the space of two years, Mao swept them away.

Party officials, helped by Red Army soldiers, went out to the villages. They called meetings and allowed the peasants to accuse the landlords of many crimes—high rents, low wages, cruelty, cheating them out of land, and other things.

The next stage was to divide the land between the peasants. The landlords who protested were sent to work on the roads or in factories.

There was some criticism and opposition. Mao handled this by taking control of all newspapers and book publishing. The Party arranged for 'self-criticism' sessions. By means of lectures and discussions, going on for hour after hour and usually at the end of a day's work, men and women were 're-educated' with the ideas of Marxism. University teachers who did not agree with the communists were sent to work with peasants in the fields.

By 1952, Mao had reached the end of the first stage of the communist take-over. All trading companies and firms owned by foreign powers were taxed so heavily that they handed over offices, warehouses and factories and left China. Most of the 9000 missionaries also left. China was cut off from Western influence and retired behind the 'bamboo curtain'.

1 In this picture, the words of the Chinese leader are brought to a distant village:
   a) Whose portrait is being held up?
   b) What is the insignia or badge on the soldiers' caps?
   c) From what you have read, make a list of the complaints that you think the peasants would have against the landlords before the Revolution.
2 In your notebook, write brief accounts of:
   a) building dams and reservoirs;
   b) Land Reform;
   c) the communes;
   d) the Hundred Flowers campaign;
   e) the Great Leap Forward.

The Communes

By 1954, Mao had realized that China's peasants were not growing enough food to feed a population of over 600 million. The next stage of the revolution was therefore to 'pool' the labour of ten or more families to work the land. The success of this scheme led to the next stage—collective farming. A local committee decided on the crops to be grown, and the villagers joined together in a team to do the work. The profits of the collective were divided between the workers according to how much time and land they had provided.

In 1958, a group of collectives were formed into a commune. By the end of the year, the work of China's peasants had been reorganized.

In the communes (some with as many as 50 000 people) the planning of farming, road-building, education and other aspects of life was organized by a committee. Where the commune did not have tractors and machinery, they used human labour to build dams and reservoirs.

The Hundred Flowers Campaign

In 1952, China began the first of the Five-Year Plans by which industry would be developed. Mao gave mining, iron and steel and food industries the highest priority. In the beginning, production was low because machinery was old and worn out. But gradually, things improved.

In 1956–7, the government declared that everyone was 'to let a hundred flowers bloom and a hundred schools of thought contend'. This meant that the Party wanted people to criticize, to say why China wasn't making faster progress. There were a lot of new ideas, but in some cities the students rioted against Party officials. The government realized that the 'hundred flowers' had led to thousands of opponents coming into the open. Suddenly, the campaign ended and the government returned to strict control over newspapers and public opinion.

The Great Leap Forward

In 1958, in the Second Five-Year Plan, the Chinese announced that industry must take giant strides, to do the work of 'twenty years in one day'. Another slogan said 'hard work for a few years, happiness for a thousand years'. More factories must be built to produce tools and machinery; dams and reservoirs were needed to control the flooding from China's great rivers. Millions of peasants dressed in blue clothes (the 'blue ants' one newspaperman called them) set to work. But dykes leaked and the steel that came from the new mills was of poor quality. Fom 1959 to 1961 China suffered three hard years which wasn't helped when the USSR withdrew all aid and the experts who had been helping. But the Great Leap was not a total failure. Production increased, great irrigation

China and her neighbours, 1978

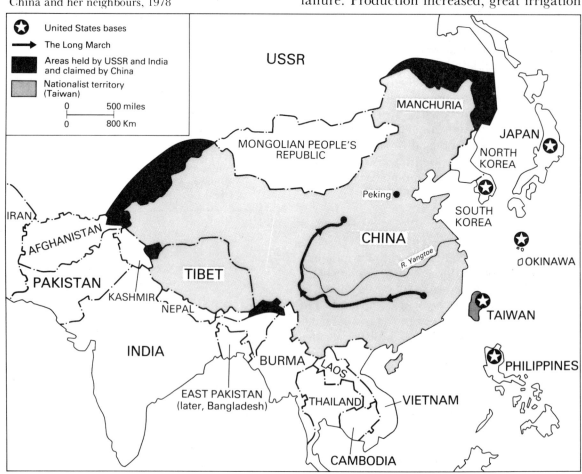

United States bases

The Long March

Areas held by USSR and India and claimed by China

Nationalist territory (Taiwan)

0   500 miles
0   800 Km

USSR

MANCHURIA

JAPAN

MONGOLIAN PEOPLE'S REPUBLIC

NORTH KOREA

Peking

SOUTH KOREA

CHINA

R. Yangtoe

OKINAWA

IRAN

AFGHANISTAN

PAKISTAN

TIBET

KASHMIR

NEPAL

TAIWAN

INDIA

BURMA

LAOS

PHILIPPINES

EAST PAKISTAN (later, Bangladesh)

THAILAND

VIETNAM

CAMBODIA

schemes were carried out and above all the Leap encouraged the Chinese to rely on self-help. They did not need outsiders, 'foreign devils' from across the sea and the mountains.

China and the World

For a long time China and the USSR were close allies. But after 1955 China claimed to be the leader of the communist world and accused the Russians of betraying the ideas of Marx. This led to a quarrel with the USSR which has not yet been mended. In 1962 China fought a short war with India when they quarrelled over frontier areas (the Chinese also say that the USSR holds land which is rightfully China's). The USA has been the biggest enemy. The Chinese helped the North Koreans to fight the USA in 1950 and supplied the North Vietnamese with weapons. The USA replied by building a ring of naval and air force bases around China.

3 Copy or trace the map of China into your notebook.
  Show the Long March and the US bases.
  Colour the countries in south-east Asia that now
  have communist governments.

The Cultural Revolution

Towards the end of the period of the Second Five-Year Plan, there was a struggle for power in China. For Mao, the revolution did not end in 1949 with victory over Chiang. Mao wanted the Chinese to become a truly classless society where everyone lived in collectives or communes and voted officials in and out of power.

But there were other leaders who Mao called the 'Rightists' or 'revisionists' (they wanted to 'revise' or change Marxist policies). They were high-ranking officials who did not think everyone should have to work in the fields. They also thought that rapid, Russian-style industrial development was needed in China, with the party officials leading the masses. In 1959, Mao was replaced by Liu Shao-chi and for a time Mao was kept in the background. Suddenly, in 1966 he emerged and began the three-year struggle called 'the cultural revolution'. This was an attempt to educate the Chinese people to his way of thinking. On the other side of the revolution were the Rightists, the party leaders like Liu and many teachers who Mao did not think gave their full support to Marxist ideas.

Millions of copies of the Little Red Book were printed. The book contained the 'Thoughts' of Mao. It became a kind of 'Bible' to guide the young people that Mao enlisted to carry on the cultural revolution. Millions of young people from 12 to 20 joined the 'Red Guards' and they preached the words of Mao across China.

In 1965, China seemed to be on the verge of a civil war. In some areas the Red Guards fought with workers. There was news of riots among the peasants, of strikes and risings. Liu Shao-chi was branded as a Rightist, and another leader emerged, Lin Piao, who in 1969 was named as Mao's successor. It appeared on the surface as if Mao had won the battle for the minds of the Chinese people. But the party officials who run China could not be overthrown. Lin Piao disappeared and was never mentioned in newspapers or seen at meetings. In 1972 it was announced that he had tried to overthrow Mao, had fled, and had been killed in an air-crash. The cultural revolution gradually died down as Mao grew older and other leaders took over.

In Mao's last years, China was ruled by a group of Communist party men. In September 1976, he died at the age of 82. There was a sudden struggle for power and Mao's widow was arrested. The new Chairman of the Party was Hua Kuo-feng.

Did the cultural revolution succeed? For a few years in the 1960s, China's workers and peasants had a real say in decision-taking. Some of these changes have lasted for more than 10 years:
- sons and daughters of workers and peasants were able to go to university;
- about 20 million Chinese moved out of the cities to work on farms;
- every civil servant or party member had to do some manual work;
- villagers were able to take a share in deciding on farming or industrial policies.

4 The Maoists told the Red Guard to 'struggle against' certain people. Who were these people?
5 Make a list of the differences that the Cultural Revolution made to life in China. Would you say that the movement was a success or a failure?

20   The Struggle for Vietnam

On Vietnam, President Johnson said:
I want to leave the footprints of America there. We're going to turn the Mekong into a Tennessee Valley.'

In 1954 the French gave up the attempt to rule Vietnam. But the American government refused to let the communists take over the south without a fight. For the next 20 years the USA poured money, weapons, and troops into South Vietnam to try to stem the communist advance. In the end they failed, the biggest American defeat in the Cold War.

The view of the American government at that time was that if one country, such as Vietnam, fell to the communists, it would knock over the neighbouring country, which would also become communist. This became known as the *domino* effect. The idea was used to explain America's struggle to prevent South Vietnam from being taken over by the forces of Ho Chi Minh.

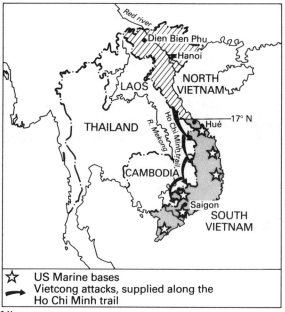

☆   US Marine bases
→   Vietcong attacks, supplied along the Ho Chi Minh trail

Vietnam

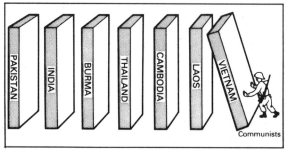
The domino effect

In 1955, Ngo Dinh Diem, who had US support, took over South Vietnam. He set up a government at Saigon, and refused to hold elections to decide whether or not the country should be reunified (as agreed at Geneva). The USA added South Vietnam to the SEATO alliance and began to pump in aid at a rate of more than 250 million dollars a year. In the north, Ho Chi Minh accepted military help from both Russia and China.

President Diem appointed members of his own family to positions within the South Vietnam government. Many of his followers were corrupt, and the government was out of touch with the peasants and the ordinary people of the towns. Many peasants secretly helped the soldiers of Ho Chi Minh who in 1960 became known as the Vietcong (Vietnamese communists). They set up hide-outs in the south, recruited local people for their army and trained them in guerrilla warfare.

Vietcong soldiers shelter in the jungle

The Americans Join In

The Americans became worried at the failure of President Diem to stop the spread of Vietcong influence in the south. In 1962 they sent more troops to advise and train the South Vietnam army. But they were still not successful in stopping the communists from growing more powerful.

In 1963 several Buddhist monks burned themselves to death in public as a protest against Diem (who was a Catholic and had persecuted some Buddhists). The Americans by now had realized that Diem was a handicap and they did nothing to prevent a revolution in November 1963 when Diem was killed. He was followed by a series of military leaders, ending with President Thieu (1967–75). None of them obtained much support from the Vietnamese people. Thieu could carry on only because of American support.

By 1965 it looked as if the communists would win. To prevent it, President Johnson decided to increase the number of American troops in Vietnam, and he sent regular army combat troops to fight the Vietcong with artillery, bombers and the most advanced form of weapons— such as flame-throwers.

 'Political power grows out of the barrel of a gun.'

Mao Tse-tung

'Agents from the North'

President Johnson declared in 1965 that the communist 'revolt' in South Vietnam would 'fizzle out' if only 'the agents from the North' could be stopped. The US Air Force carried out one bombing raid after another on Hanoi and other North Korean cities. Far from stopping the guerrilla war in the south, the raids led to more attacks on Saigon and other cities. The USSR and China increased their assistance for North Korea. In the communist world the war was called 'a struggle for liberation' and by 1965 there were over 250000 'agents of the North' fighting in South Vietnam.

 We have the enemy on the ropes, and another 200000 GIs will finish him off.'

General Westmoreland, US Commander-in-Chief in Vietnam 1968

---

1 Draw a map of Vietnam. Show the main cities—Saigon, Hanoi, Hué, Dien Bien Phu; the Red and the Mekong rivers; South and North Vietnam, and the line of Ho Chi Minh Trail.
2 Explain, by means of a diagram, what was meant by the 'domino theory'.

---

3 Write sentences to explain:
  a) why 'the agents from the North' could not be defeated
  b) why the Vietcong received so much support from the people of South Vietnam
  c) why the Americans increased the number of troops sent to fight in Vietnam.

A US marine grapples with a Vietcong soldier
April 1968

'The Enemy is on the Ropes'

When President Johnson took over from Kennedy in 1963 he decided to quell the revolt by tough measures. By 1968 there were over 500000 American troops in Vietnam, and the 'carpet bombing' of the North was stepped up. The full horror of modern warfare was let loose on Vietnam. Napalm and chemical warfare (including poison that killed trees and crops) were used throughout South Vietnam. The country was in such chaos that American troops could not tell the Vietcong from peaceful Vietnamese. Villages that gave shelter to communists were burned to the ground. In one of the most shocking massacres, American troops mercilessly killed men, women and children at the village of My Lai in March 1968. Yet the Vietcong survived, and indeed their strength increased. In 1968 an attack was launched on several key towns. For a few hours the American Embassy at Saigon was captured by the Vietcong. The city of Hué was largely destroyed to the two-month Tet offensive.

400 in mass killings

SAIGON, 9 March
THE Vietcong killed over 400 civilians during the 26 days it occupied the northern Vietnamese city of Hué, the American Embassy said in Saigon today.

The mass killings, reported by eyewitnesses, had been substantiated by reports from the combined interrogation centre at Hué.

The figure included 100 found in three mass graves with their hands tied behind their backs. Women and children were among them.

According to reports, a Vietcong unit assembled 200 South Vietnamese civilian prisoners five miles east of Hué. They marched the prisoners to the nearby town of Tom Nam Duong, took 75 of them to a nearby rice paddy and shot them.

The Observer 10 March 1968

4 Look at the picture of Hué and read the account of the atrocities in the newspaper article. Describe the damage you can see at Hué. Find out, and describe, what happened when *napalm* and *defoliants* were used as weapons. Explain why both the Americans (at My Lai and other places) and the Vietcong carried out *atrocities* on civilians.

Hué, once a beautiful city, left in ruins after an attack

'Down with the Vietnam War!'

In the 1960s more and more people raised their voices to protest about the Vietnam War. In the USA they were, at first, students, blacks and do-gooders. The protesters were accused of being disloyal to the USA or were said to be on the side of the 'commies'. However, the cruelty of the war (brought to Americans by news broadcasts on television) and the increasing number of American casualties (500 a week in 1968), led to more people asking why the USA should fight in Vietnam.

By the end of 1968 the protest movement had grown so noisy that President Johnson reduced the bombing of South Vietnam and said he would not stand again for election. The new President, Nixon, tried a different policy. The South Vietnam army, re-armed and re-trained, would take over from American troops. But at the same time President Nixon ordered the bombing of North Vietnam to be resumed. The protests in America now grew more violent. The police had to break up student riots, and at one demonstration four students were shot dead by the National Guard.

For the next three years the war dragged on, and despite the fact that US combat troops were gradually withdrawn, over 15000 men were killed or wounded. Peace negotiations began in 1972, but when the discussions broke down, Nixon ordered the bombing of North Vietnam to start again. In 1973 a peace agreement was signed at Paris and at last the Americans had an excuse to escape from Vietnam. But the war went on for another two years. Finally, in 1975, the Vietcong swept through the south and in April the city of Saigon was captured and re-named Ho Chi Minh City (six years after the death of the communist leader). Therefore, after 30 years of war, 43000 American casualties and an unknown number of Vietnamese killed, the country fell to the communists. By then, too, Laos and Cambodia also had communist governments.

American ex-soldiers, who had fought in the Vietnam war, join the protest against it in 1969

5 This time-chart shows the main stages in the Vietnam War. Copy it into your book, and add two more stages in the right places:
1954 fall of city of Dien Bien Phu to communists
1964 USA begins bombing North Vietnam

Time chart

1942 Japanese invade and drive French from Indo-China
1943 Ho Chi Minh leads fight against Japanese
1945 French return
1946 Beginning of communist revolt against French
1954 Geneva Conference
1960 Vietcong intensify war
1965 anti-war movement in USA gains strength
1968 the Tet offensive by Vietcong against major cities
1973 Paris peace treaty
1975 North Korean forces overrun South Vietnam

21 India and Pakistan

In the Second World War, Indian troops fought bravely in British armies serving in Europe, Africa and in Burma. For many years before the war, Indian nationalists led by Gandhi and Nehru had been demanding Indian independence. In 1945, at the end of the war, the cry was heard again for India to be allowed to go its own way.

But the problem was complicated by India's religious differences. About a quarter of India's population were Muslim. Hundreds of years ago, Muslim warriors had conquered and ruled India, lording it over the Hindus. Ali Mohammed Jinnah, the leader of the Muslims, feared that when India became independent, the Hindus would swamp the proud Muslims. He therefore demanded that the British should partition India into two areas—one for Muslims, one for Hindus. He said that a new state of Pakistan should be set up for all Muslims who wanted to live free from Indian domination.

In 1945 the new Labour government in Britain declared that India would shortly be given its full independence. Lord Mountbatten was sent to India as Viceroy to organize the British handover. He decided on 15 August 1947 as Independence Day. The Muslim and Hindu leaders, however, could not agree. Gandhi wanted a united India, Jinnah was determined on partition. Rioting and fighting broke out in 1946 between the two religious groups but Mountbatten said that the date of independence would not be changed.

Gandhi at a meeting

Gandhi was the main leader of the Indian nationalist movement. Born in 1869, he studied law in London and for many years he lived in South Africa. At the age of 45 he returned to India. He became the leader of the Indian Congress Party. Its policy was to make India completely independent of the British. Gandhi was also a religious leader. He lived very simply and travelled about the country, taking prayer meetings. He was put in prison many times by the British. When independence came in 1947, there was rioting and war in India. Gandhi tried to calm it. In January 1948 he was murdered by a fanatic.

People lie dead in a street in the city of Calcutta after a riot, 1946

Independence and War

In 1947, the plan was that in areas such as the Punjab and Bengal, where the two religions were mixed, a commission would draw boundary lines.

But when independence finally came, the two groups fought each other in the streets and in the fields. In the Punjab, the Sikhs refused to allow their state to be divided up, and so they fought and killed hundreds of Muslims. Thousands of innocent people died in the fighting. Over six million Muslim refugees fled into Pakistan, and over four million Hindus crossed into India. There was chaos, panic and fear. In despair, Mahatma Gandhi went to Delhi to try to stop the riots, but he was murdered. Then the Pakistan army invaded Kashmir to stop the ruler from handing over his land to India. Indian troops rushed to Kashmir and for years the province was torn by fighting between the two sides. In the years that followed, the fighting died down. But in Pakistan, divided into two areas in the east and the west (*see the map*), there were terrible problems of poverty, disease and lack of education to be faced.

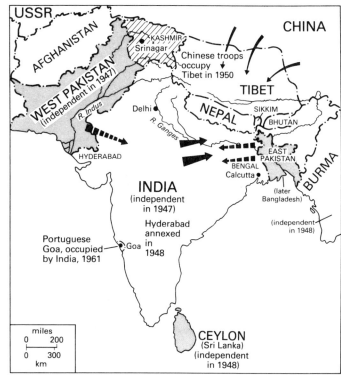

Indian independence

 Muslims can expect neither justice nor fair play under a Congress Government of Hindus.'

Jinnah

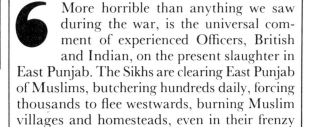 More horrible than anything we saw during the war, is the universal comment of experienced Officers, British and Indian, on the present slaughter in East Punjab. The Sikhs are clearing East Punjab of Muslims, butchering hundreds daily, forcing thousands to flee westwards, burning Muslim villages and homesteads, even in their frenzy burning their own.'

Ian Morrison (war correspondent to *The Times*) 1947

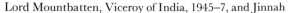

Lord Mountbatten, Viceroy of India, 1945–7, and Jinnah

1 Write out the beginning of this sentence, and add your own ending:
   'In 1947 the British had to partition India into different countries because ....
   ....'
2 Make a list of the *results* of the creation of India and Pakistan as two separate states.
3 Draw or trace a map of India to show what happened in 1947–8 in India, Burma, Ceylon, Pakistan and Kashmir.

The New India

Jawaharlal Nehru was India's first Prime Minister. He was determined that India should become an industrial nation. But one of his first problems was to deal with the princes who ruled large areas of India. He bought them off with money and pensions except in Hyderabad where the ruler wanted to be independent. Troops were sent in and Hyderabad was incorporated into India.

Nehru set up a form of government modelled on the British system with a parliament (the Lok Sabha) elected by the votes of all adult Indians. The Congress party dominated all other parties and formed the first government.

One of the biggest problems was to grow enough food. India in 1961 had a population of 434 millions which was increasing fast as disease was brought under control. (It had risen to 605 millions by 1976.) Eighty per cent of the people lived in the countryside, and when there were floods or droughts, they starved. Nehru faced a huge task because India did not have enough money to invest in industry, irrigation and modern farming methods. He borrowed from other nations and received help from the United Nations, but the population continued to increase faster than the food supply. Poor and starving people poured into cities and towns and thousands took to sleeping on the streets because they had nowhere else to go.

In a Calcutta street

Nehru, Prime Minister of India, 1948–1964

The Five-Year Plans

Nehru tried the Russian method of planning. The first Five-Year Plan (1951–6) tackled farming, the second dealt with industry. There was some improvement, but because prices rose, millions suffered from poverty and hunger.

Goa, Kashmir and China

The Indians were irritated that Goa was still owned by Portugal (*see the map*). In 1961, Nehru sent troops to seize the town. In Kashmir, United Nations soldiers patrolled a cease-fire line. The dispute between India and Pakistan dragged on for years until in 1966 a settlement was agreed on. Nehru kept India free from alliances with the USA or USSR. For a time he was friendly with China. But in 1950 Chinese troops occupied Tibet and in 1959 the religious leader, the Dalai Lama, fled to India. The Chinese claimed a frontier area and in 1962 attacked and defeated Indian troops on the border. In

the brief war that followed, India had to give way.

Nehru died in 1964. Two years later, his daughter, Mrs Indira Gandhi, became Prime Minister. She introduced many changes but her attempts to make Hindi the official language and to bring in compulsory birth control were unpopular. The Congress party gradually lost support and Mrs Gandhi resigned. In 1977 a new government under Mr Desai took over.

Pakistan

In 1948, Pakistan was made up two areas, separated by a thousand miles. West Pakistan was a dry, arid region with mountains, deserts and the valley of the river Indus. East Pakistan, in the delta of the river Ganges, where rice and jute are grown, was a vastly different area. Cyclones and floods bring death and destruction to the millions of people who live there (100 000 died in the floods of 1970). From the start of Pakistan, it was very difficult to weld the two regions together into one nation.

Another problem was that Pakistan could not find a settled form of government. Mohammed Ali Jinnah, the creator of Pakistan, died in 1948. Three years later his successor was assassinated. After internal unrest, riots and disturbances, the army took over under General Ayub Khan as President. He ruled for some years and led Pakistan into the alliances (the Baghdad Pact and SEATO) of the western nations. But unrest and riots in 1969 forced Ayub Khan to resign, and he was succeeded by other army leaders.

In 1970, Ali Bhutto won a big victory in West Pakistan's elections and for a time he established a form of democratic government. But in East Pakistan, Sheikh Rahman demanded a free country and he broke away to form a new country—Bangladesh. In March 1971 the army generals of West Pakistan decided to put down this rising by force. The result was a civil war and millions of Bengal people fled across the border into India. Mr Bhutto in turn fell from power, was put into prison, and later executed. Once again Pakistan fell under the control of army generals.

Kashmir: the picture shows Sringar the capital. Most Kashmiris are Muslim, but the state had a Hindu ruler and this caused trouble between India and Pakistan

Mrs Indira Gandhi

4 Make a list of the problems of
  a) India
  and
  b) Pakistan
  since independence.
5 In your notebook, write a paragraph about each of these leaders:
  a) Mahatma Gandhi;
  b) Nehru;
  c) Mrs Indira Gandhi;
  d) Ayub Khan.

Index